# A. Wallace Rimington's
# *Colour-Music*

Wildside Press

Selected by Michael Betancourt.
Copyright © 2004 by Michael Betancourt, all rights reserved.

Original Publication:

*A New Art: 'Colour-Music'*
A paper read at St. James's Hall on June 6, 1895, published in pamphlet form by Messrs. Spottiswoode & Co., New St. Square, June 13, 1895.

*Colour-Music: The Art of Mobile Colour*
A book published by Hutchinson & Company, Paternoster Row, London, 1912.

Wildside Press
www.wildsidepress.com

# CONTENTS

The United States Patent for the *Colour Organ* (1894) . . . . . . . . . 7

A New Art: 'Colour-Music' (1895) . . . . . . . . . . . . . . . . . . 43

*Colour-Music:*
*The Art of Mobile Colour*

Author's Preface . . . . . . . . . . . . . . . . . . . . . . . . . .
Introductory Note by Sir Hubert von Herkomer . . . . . . . . . . .
Note by Dr. W. Brown . . . . . . . . . . . . . . . . . . . . . . .

1: Introduction A Mobile Colour Art . . . . . . . . . . . . . . . . 67
2: The Uses of Colour-Music . . . . . . . . . . . . . . . . . . . . 73
3: Resemblances Between Music & Mobile Colour . . . . . . . . . 78
4: The Colour Scale & Mobile Colour . . . . . . . . . . . . . . . . 82
5: Points of Analogy Between Sound & Colour . . . . . . . . . . 102
6: Construction of Colour-Organ & Other Instruments . . . . . . . 115
7: Effects Produced by Colour-Music . . . . . . . . . . . . . . . 133
8: The Colour-Sense & Its Decay . . . . . . . . . . . . . . . . . 154
9: The Emotional Influences of Colour . . . . . . . . . . . . . . 172
10: The Educational Influences of Colour-Music . . . . . . . . . . 184
11: Mobile Colour & The Artist . . . . . . . . . . . . . . . . . . 193
12: Some Scientific Opinions . . . . . . . . . . . . . . . . . . . 203
13: Remarks Upon Criticisms & Appreciations of Colour-Music . . 215
14: Some Further Remarks & Some Past Proposals . . . . . . . . 237
15: Color-Music & Psychology . . . . . . . . . . . . . . . . . . 248

Appendix . . . . . . . . . . . . . . . . . . . . . . . . . . . . . 261

About the Author . . . . . . . . . . . . . . . . . . . . . . . . . 275

# United States Patent Office.

ALEXANDER WALLACE RIMINGTON,
OF LONDON ENGLAND.

METHOD OF AND APPARATUS FOR
PRODUCING COLOR EFFECTS.

SPECIFICATION forming part of Letters
Patent No. 547,359, dated October 1,1895.

Application filed July 16,1894.
Serial No, 517,745. (No model.)

To all whom it may concern:

Be it known that I, ALEXANDER WALLACE REMINGTON, a subject of the Queen of Great Britain and Ireland, residing at 26 Kensington Park Gardens, Bayswater, in the county of London, England, have invented a Method of and Apparatus for Producing Color Effects, of which the following is a specification.

According to this invention colored light is projected onto a screen or other suitable body or surface in such a manner as to give effects in color, bearing a more or less definite relationship to certain sound-vibrations. This may be effected in a variety of ways, such as by employing a keyboard with appropriate mechanism to control devices, such as diaphragms, adapted to arrest or permit rays of light to pass from any suitable source onto the screen or other object on which the color effects are to be produced, such rays of light being projected through suitable colored media onto the said screen or other object. Thus it will be understood that by this invention, inter alia, sound-music may, figuratively speaking, be translated into color-music. In order to throw colored light upon a screen or other suitable object according to the novel method set forth, apparatus variously constructed and arranged can, as already indicated, be employed. An arrangement for the purpose may comprise, for example, a keyboard arranged in any convenient manner—as, for instance, it may be similar to that of a pianoforte or organ, this keyboard being connected by a series of trackers or wires with a corresponding set of diaphragms, adjusted and balanced by weights or otherwise, arranged in front of a number of reflectors and lenses, and a set of colored glasses, films, or spectroscopic prisms, arranged in such a manner as to color the light reflected from the mirrors on passing through the lenses, there being in connection therewith special fittings with suitable sources of light, such as arc electric lamps or oxyhydrogen lamps. As an additional feature I in some cases also make provision for the introduction of the element of variable form and intensity into the rays of light passing through the corresponding color medium and the color space or image thus produced upon the screen Apparatus constructed and arranged in any convenient form to operate on the principle of this invention can be used, figuratively speaking, to translate sound-music into color-music by such adjustment of individual colors of the spectrum upon the said glass or other diaphragms in regard to the sound-vibrations to which they correspond as approximately to correspond also with the relative air-vibrations of the chromatic scale as such is understood in music. In other words, according to the just-indicated application of this invention, each note of the keyboard will be connected with a color whose place in the spectrum will correspond in a certain mathematical sense with the place occupied by a note upon the chromatic sound-scale of the musical instrument.

    The invention is also applicable, by arranging the said colors and notes or keys of the keyboard to correspond with any other arbitrary scale which may be desired, for the purpose of producing other forms of color-music or carrying out color experiments. By suitable modifications of certain features in carrying out the invention it can be adapted to meet the requirements of color measurement and notation for artistic and art industrial purposes. The mode of effecting this will be readily understood when it is remembered that the process admits of notation exactly as in the case of music.

In order to facilitate the use of the apparatus, the keys of the keyboard may be also colored to correspond with the respective colors projected upon the screen by lenses or reflectors. The accompanying drawings illustrate, by way of example, a construction of apparatus for carrying my invention into effect. In the drawings, Figure 1 shows a front elevation of the apparatus, partly in section. Fig. 2 shows parts of the apparatus in vertical section in a plane at right angles to Fig. 1. Fig. 3 is also a vertical section in a plane at right angles to Fig. 1, but is, like other views hereinafter referred to, drawn to a larger scale. This view shows one of the front apertures 6 and the arrangement with respect to it of the corresponding lamp 17, condenser 18, lens 19, and set of diaphragms 5, connected to the keyboard, as also the arrangements for supporting and adjusting the lamp, condenser, and lens. Fig. 4 is a detached view at right angles to Fig. 3, showing the means illustrated in that figure for supporting and adjusting the lamp and other parts. Fig. 5 shows, in front elevation, a set of diaphragms with their holders, actuating-wires, springs, buffer-stop, and other parts hereinafter described. Fig. 6 is a view, partly in section, at right angles to Fig. 5. Fig. 7 shows, to a larger scale, a wire loop 55 and a wire 53, which is connected, as hereinafter described, to a diaphragm-holder, and is furnished with an adjustable nut or button 57, so that downward movement of the loop 55 will, through the button 57 and wire 53, actuate the corresponding diaphragm-holder, and that the wire 53 can move downward without actuating the loop 55. Fig. 8 shows in plan the construction of the registers through which the wires 53 and loops 55, respectively, work. Fig. 9 shows, to a larger scale than Fig. 6, a series of diaphragm holders, together with attached, connected, and adjacent parts hereinafter more particularly referred to. Figs. 10 and 11 are detail views of the adjusting-screw arrangement shown to a smaller scale at 29 in Fig. 3. Fig. 12 is a detail view of the arrangement, shown to a smaller scale in Fig. 3, for adjusting the distance of the lamp from the front of the apparatus along the upper part of frame 25. Fig. 13 is a detail view of the arrangement, shown to a smaller scale in Fig. 3, for enabling the position of the lamp to be adjusted in a lateral sense. Figs.14 and 15 are views, at right angles to one another, of the adjustable eyepiece employed to facilitate accurate adjustment of the lamp-are, notwithstanding irregularities in the combustion of the carbons.

1 is a keyboard, similar to that of an ordinary organ, from which the movement of the keys is conveyed, by means of stickers and trackers and the back fall 2, to the rollers 3, which rollers transfer the movement, in the manner usual in an organ, to the trackers 56. These trackers actuate the diaphragms 38, of which there is a series opposite each front aperture 6, (see Figs. 1, 2, 3, 5, 6, and 9,) in such manner as to cause the said diaphragms to rise and fall or oscillate in front of the apertures 6, so that the respective diaphragms will be opposite to the corresponding apertures or not, according as the corresponding keys of the keyboard are for the time being elevated or depressed.

It is advisable to make the diaphragms of some material that is strong, light, and capable of enduring high temperatures. I have obtained satisfactory results by using thin pieces of mica, and in order to obviate noise, which I found liable to occur when employing a single thickness, I construct each diaphragm of two layers or films secured in one and the same diaphragm-holder, so as to be held in con tact, with one another. The said diaphragms are colored with the respective colors referred to above, or tinted gray, or otherwise adapted to absorb a portion of the light sent through them, as hereinafter described, the object being to enable any given note or key to allow the given strength of a certain color to pass the corresponding aperture 6 and appear upon a screen or other suitable object placed in front of the instrument. That diaphragm of each series which is nearest to the corresponding aperture 6 is rendered non-transparent by being smoked and varnished, or may be made of a thin plate of metal or other suitable material. An arrangement is provided, as hereinafter explained, by which, on the depression of any given note of the octave, this non-transparent diaphragm is removed simultaneously with, any other diaphragm or diaphragms of the series belonging to the same aperture 6, the object being that on the depression of any given key this non-transparent diaphragm shall invariably be moved from the front of its aperture 6, so as to allow the cone of light rays from the corresponding lamp to pass through such aperture.

In addition to the movable diaphragms 5 there is a stationary diaphragm fixed immediately in front of the non-transparent diaphragm, and, whether the other movable diaphragm be colored or be tinted gray or otherwise rendered absorbent of light, this fixed diaphragm is invariably colored of the tint which corresponds to the given note upon the keyboard.

For the transparent colored diaphragms it. is important to use transparent colors and varnishes capable of withstanding the high temperature and powerful light. As the result of numerous experiments, I have found it advantageous to use what is known as " Soehn6's No. 3 varnish" and various colors of aniline origin, such as aurine, mixing the color and varnish in proportions depending no upon the depth of color required, applying the varnish so colored to the mica or glass diaphragm in the same way that a photographer covers a photographic plate with collodion, and drying afterward by artificial heat. When I have failed to obtain the particular color desired, I have used, in lieu of juxtaposed colored films of mica, a piece of colored glass having, as nearly as possible, the color desired, and I have corrected the color by the use of a superimposed tint of colored varnish such as already described. In these eases the mica diaphragms, tinted gray or otherwise rendered partially non-transparent to light, have merely served to partially resist the passage of the light or to allow more or less of it to pass, for which reason such diaphragms may conveniently be called, for distinction, "absorption" diaphragms, the color being given by the one fixed plate of glass.

39 are the diaphragm-holders. They are made as light as possible. They may be of any suitable material. I have used mahogany with satisfactory results.

Referring to Pigs. 5 to 9, the holders constituting a series are pivoted upon a rod or center 40, so as to be capable of oscillation in the direction indicated by the dotted lines 41. 5 7 is the fixed diaphragm. It is carried by the nipping block 42.

43 is a perforated metal plate attached to the face of the diaphragm-board 44 ad determining the effective area of the aperture 6, which may be of any desired shape.

44a is a buffer-block, to which is attached a piece of thick felt 45, which receives the impact of any diaphragm-holder 39 when thrown back by the depression of a note of the keyboard.

46 is a block or bracket accurately grooved to take the diaphragm-holders 39, which are mounted upon the steel center-pin 40, upon which they oscillate.

50 are arms formed of wire, (it may be brass wire,) each securely attached to a diaphragm-holder 39 and bent horizontally so as to extend across the back of the diaphragm or diaphragms at the inner side of that to which it is secured, the arrangement being such that upon the outermost diaphragm being moved it will carry the remaining three with it. Upon the second diaphragm being moved it will carry the two at its inner side, and so on. 51 and 52 are registers or guides constructed as shown in Fig.

8. Both these registers or guides are "clothed" to prevent noise and friction. 53 are wires each bent to a right angle at its upper part, so as to engage in a hole at 54 in the corresponding diaphragm-holder.

Each of these wires is actuated by a wire loop 55 attached to a tracker 56. Upon each wire 53 there is a not or button 57, so that when the tracker is actuated so as to pull down a wire loop 55 the corresponding wire 53 will be pulled down; bat that upon any given diaphragm being moved the remaining wires, which are depressed by others of the diaphragm-holders simultaneously moved, may pass freely through their respective holes at the tops of the loops 55. The diaphragm-holders 39 and the wires 53 are held in position by springs 58, which are regulated by the nuts or buttons 59.

In order to overcome the slight disadvantage resulting from having to move a number of diaphragms and springs by the depression of one note in the upper octaves, and in order also to be able to increase the size of the diaphragms, if desired, without throwing undue stress on the notes of the keyboard, I may in some cases attach to the trackers a pneumatic arrangement such as is sometimes employed in organs. Behind the aperture 6 are placed the lamps or other suitable sources of light and the lenses whereby to project cones of light-rays through the apertures.

In the arrangement illustrated (see Fig. 3) 17 is a self-focusing electric-arc lamp, but there may be substituted an oxycalcium burner or other suitable source of illumination. 18 is a condenser and 19 a lens through which the light is carried to the aperture 6. 20 is a screw engaging in a nut 21, which is carried by the rods 22 and plate 23. The screw 20 is for the purpose of raising or lowering the table 24, which carries the condenser and lens. This table and the arc-lamp 17 are 75 carried by the frame 25, which rests upon the wooden support 27 and is also supported by the T-shaped bar 28, forming part of the general framing of the instrument. The upper portion of the frame 25 is pivoted at 28 and 80 can be raised or lowered by the screw 29, Figs. 10 and 11. This is to provide for the accurate adjustment of the carbon-points of the arc-lamp 17 opposite the condenser 18. Adjustment of the lamp in a direction from front 85 to back of the apparatus is provided for by the screw 30, (see Fig. 12,) which is attached to the blocks 31, adapted to slide on the top of the frame and carry the lamp-pivots 32. Lateral adjustment is provided for by providing the frame 25, which is pivoted at 27*, with a slot and pinching-screw 33. (See Fig. 13.) The pivoted frame 25 slides upon the bar 28. In order to facilitate this lateral adjustment, to enable the carbon-arc to be accurately adjusted and kept in proper position, notwithstanding any irregularities in the combustion of the carbon-points, there is provided an eyepiece 34, Figs. 14 and 15. It can be raised and lowered upon the rod 35, and the small 100 slit 36 is capable of being rendered as narrow as may be desired by the small metal slide 37, which is made to fit tightly upon the front plate of the eyepiece or gage.

It is to be understood that the various adjusting devices herein before mentioned are provided in order that the cones or beams of light passing through the various openings 6 may be projected wholly or partially onto one and the same portion of a screen or other body, in order that the resultant color effect produced on such screen or body shall be that due to the combination of all the beams or cones of light projected at any given time.

Where it is desired to enable (a) glasses upon which forms produced by sound-vibrations or by photography, drawing, or painting, or (6) glasses of varying transparency to be shifted across the paths of the cones of light-rays, so as to increase or diminish the r2o quantity of colored light projected upon the screen or other suitable object, the following arrangement may be conveniently employed.

Referring to Figs. 1 and 2, immediately in front of the diaphragms, or it may be in front of the lenses behind the apertures 6,1 arrange a series of frames 8, which are carried upon brackets 9, or upon other suitable supports, and are adapted to be shifted from side to side by means of the stops 10 or pedal 11, and to return to a fixed position, by springs 12 or equivalent means, on the stop or stops being replaced or on the pedal being released.

These frames 8 are each fitted with panes of glass, the number of which corresponds to that of the apertures 6 opposite which the frame is placed, the portion of each pane that is normally opposite an aperture being plain, 5 so as to have no effect on a beam of light passing through it, while the remaining portion is of the nature mentioned under a or & and is brought opposite the opening by moving the frame to the right. In front of the frame ro 8 is an outer casing 13, which carries a series of projecting funnels li, corresponding in position with the apertures 6, these funnels having for object to prevent any escape of light sideways from behind the diaphragms. The 15 space 15 is or may be occupied by an American organ or harmonium actuated by the same keyboard that actuates the diaphragms 5. In this way both light and sound music may conveniently be played at the same time and the color-organ will be enabled the better to be accompanied by other sound instruments or an orchestra, &c.

With regard to the form to be introduced by means of the sliding frames above referred to, I may mention that I have employed the kind of forms produced by sound known as the "Watts-Hughes voice pictures," photographs of cloud-forms, and other objects. My invention is susceptible of various applications. One of these is the direct production, by means of the keyboard, from music written for an instrument such as the organ or pianoforte, of what I call "color-music," by which expression I desire to have it understood that I mean color effects produced upon a screen or other suitable object, and which are variable in point of combination, intensity, tint, and rapidity of change in the same way that in sound-music given notes are variable in point of combination, intensity, tone, and rapidity of change, at the will of the executive musician. In this connection it will be evident that by my invention I am enabled to associate time and rhythm with color and an almost infinite number of varying combinations of color in the same way that the almost infinite number of sound combinations may be obtained by means of known sound-instruments, such as the organ or piano; or color-music may be produced as a separate composition and independently of sound-music, though accompanied by it in some cases on other instruments or an orchestra.

My apparatus can also be constructed in such a manner as to express or take advantage of the remarkable analogy which exists between the prismatic spectrum of white light and the musical scale. In the case of the spectrum, the lowest visible color in the red portion of the spectrum-band approximately corresponds to a rate of four hundred and fifty-one millions of millions of vibrations per second, and the highest visible color in the violet portion to a rate of seven hundred and eighty-five millions of millions of vibrations per second or, roughly, double that of the red portion.

Taking any tonic note—say, C—on the sound or musical scale, the corresponding note at the top of the octave has double the number of air-vibrations per second, and if we suppose the said tonic note to correspond with the extreme red of the spectrum and the seventh musical note, or note immediately below the upper tonic, to correspond to the extreme violet of the spectrum, we have the closest possible analogy, in point of ratio of vibration, between the color-octave of the spectrum and the sound-octave of the musical scale.

In one form of my instrument the intervals between the colors, taking them in point of position along the spectrum-band and their ratio of vibration, have been arranged upon the same chromatic and diatonic system as that of the notes of the musical scale, the octave being completed by the recurrence of the red, toward which the blue end of the spectrum would seem to tend, by the gradual conversion of the blue into violet, this upper red note thus recurring as the tonic recurs in the final note of the musical octave, and the relative ratio of vibration of the other notes being in an identical relationship on both the color-scale of this "color-organ," as it may be called, and any properly-tuned sound-organ or pianoforte. With this object in view, the color of the diaphragms used in my " color - organ," as I call it, are obtained, when it is used for this musical purpose, by calculating the approximate ratio of vibration at proper intervals along the whole length of the spectrum, projected upon a white screen and matching the color at the required points, corresponding in respect of the ratio of vibration to the notes of the musical scale. This is done by cutting off by a suitable slit, as understood in connection with the spectroscope, a narrow band of color at these respective points or intervals, and experimentally varying the color of the diaphragm by the use of various coloring agents, such as hereinbefore referred to, or by means of superimposed tinted glasses, until on passing a beam of white light through it a similar color band or indication is obtained or projected upon the spectrum-screen, corresponding in tint to that of the above-mentioned narrow band of color.

Another application of my invention is for the production of color effects entirely independently of sound-musical relationship, for stage and other purposes. It may also be used for experimenting upon and notation of combinations of colors for artistic, scientific, or manufacturing purposes.

What I claim is—

1. A method of producing color effects such as herein above referred to as "color music" which consists in causing separate and differently colored beams of light to be projected in a more or less intermittent and variable manner upon a screen or other object so as to wholly or partly coincide thereon and produce color effects that are variable in point of combination, intensity, tint and rapidity of change.

2. A method of producing color effects such as herein above referred to as "color music," which consists in causing beams of light to pass through separate and differently colored media, varying the intensity of the colored beams of light thus obtained, and causing said colored beams of light to be projected in a more or less intermittent manner and in variable numbers at a time wholly or partly upon the same portion of a screen or other object so as to produce color effects thereon that are variable in point of combination, intensity, tint and rapidity of change, as set forth.

3. A method of producing color effects such as herein above referred to as "color music," consisting in causing one, two or more of a series of beams of light the colors of which correspond to numbers of light vibrations having approximately the same ratio to each other as that of the numbers of air vibrations corresponding to the notes upon the chromatic sound scale of a musical instrument, as herein set forth, to be projected in a more or less intermittent and variable manner upon a common portion of a screen or other object so as to thereby produce all the effects of rhythm or time as in sound music.

4. For producing color effects such as herein above referred to as "color music," apparatus comprising a source of light, appropriately colored media arranged in the paths of converging beams of light traveling from said source in a direction such that the several beams or portions of each will fall upon a portion of a screen or

other object common to them, movable non-transparent diaphragms whereby the said beams of light or parts thereof can at will be arrested or allowed to travel from said source of light through said colored media in a regulated manner and be combined on said screen or other object and keys and connecting mechanism adapted to operate said non-transparent diaphragms, as set forth.

5. For producing color effects such as herein referred to as "color music," apparatus comprising means for converging beams of light or parts thereof onto a common portion of a screen or other object, appropriately colored media and absorption diaphragms arranged in the paths of said converging beams of light, opaque diaphragms whereby the said beams can be arrested or projected at will, and keys and connecting mechanism whereby said absorption and opaque diaphragms can be operated in any desired order substantially as herein described for the purposes specified.

6. For producing color effects such as herein above referred to as "color music," apparatus comprising a source of light, means for converging two or more beams of light or parts thereof from said source onto a common portion of a screen or other object, appropriately colored media arranged in the paths of said converging beams of light, opaque diaphragms whereby the said beams of light can at will be arrested, or projected in a regulated manner from said source of light through said colored media and wholly or in part combined on said screen or other object keys and connecting mechanism where by said opaque diaphragms can be operated, variable effect diaphragms adapted to be interposed in the paths of said beams, and means for moving said variable effect diaphragms into and out of the paths of said beams, substantially as herein described for the purpose specified.

7. For producing color effects, apparatus comprising lamps, condensers and lenses whereby converging beams of light can be projected from said lamps onto a screen or

other object so as to wholly or partially overlap each other thereon, colored and opaque diaphragms normally arranged in the paths of said beams, and keys and connecting mechanism whereby said opaque diaphragm can be operated in a systematic manner, substantially as herein described for the purpose specified.

8. For producing color effects, apparatus comprising lamps, condensers and lenses for projecting converging beams of light from said lamps onto a screen or other object so as wholly or partially to overlap one another thereon, colored and opaque diaphragms normally arranged in the paths of said beams, keys and connecting mechanism whereby said opaque diaphragms can be operated in a systematic manner, variable effect diaphragms adapted to be moved across the paths of said beams, and means for operating said variable effect diaphragms, substantially as herein described.

9. For producing color effects, apparatus comprising a casing formed with a number of apertures, lamps arranged behind said apertures, condensers and lenses arranged between said lamp and apertures, means for independently adjusting the position of each center of light and each combined condenser and lens, sets of diaphragms arranged opposite said apertures and each consisting of a fixed colored diaphragm, a set of movable absorption diaphragms, and a movable opaque diaphragm, a key board, and mechanism connecting each of the keys of said key-board with one of the movable absorption diaphragms, and the opaque diaphragm of the corresponding set of movable diaphragms substantially as herein described for the purposes specified.

10. For producing color effects, apparatus comprising a casing formed with a number of apertures, lamps arranged behind said apertures, condensers and lenses arranged between said lamp and apertures, means for independently adjusting the position of each center of light and each combined condenser and lens, sets of dia-

phragms arranged opposite said apertures and each consisting of a fixed colored diaphragm, a set of movable absorption diaphragms, and a movable opaque diaphragm, a key board, mechanism connecting each of the keys of said keyboard with one of the movable absorption diaphragms and the opaque diaphragm of the corresponding set of movable diaphragms sliding frames carrying variable effect diaphragms, and means for bringing the latter diaphragms opposite said apertures substantially as herein described for the purposes specified.

In testimony whereof I have signed my name to this specification in the presence of two subscribing witnesses.
    ALEXANDER WALLACE RIMINGTON.

Witnesses:
    W. B. WILBERFORCE,
    H. HEATHER.

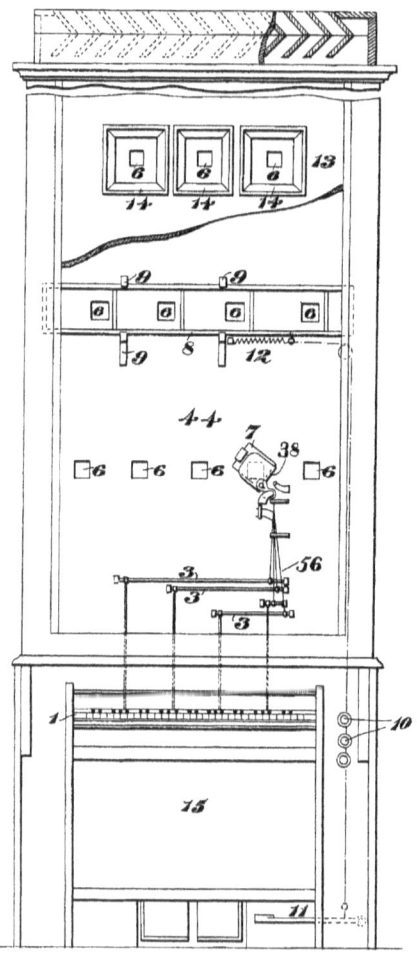

*Figure 1.*

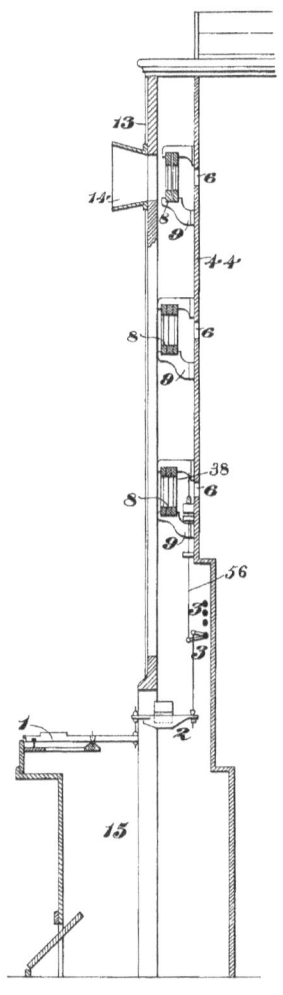

*Figure 2.*

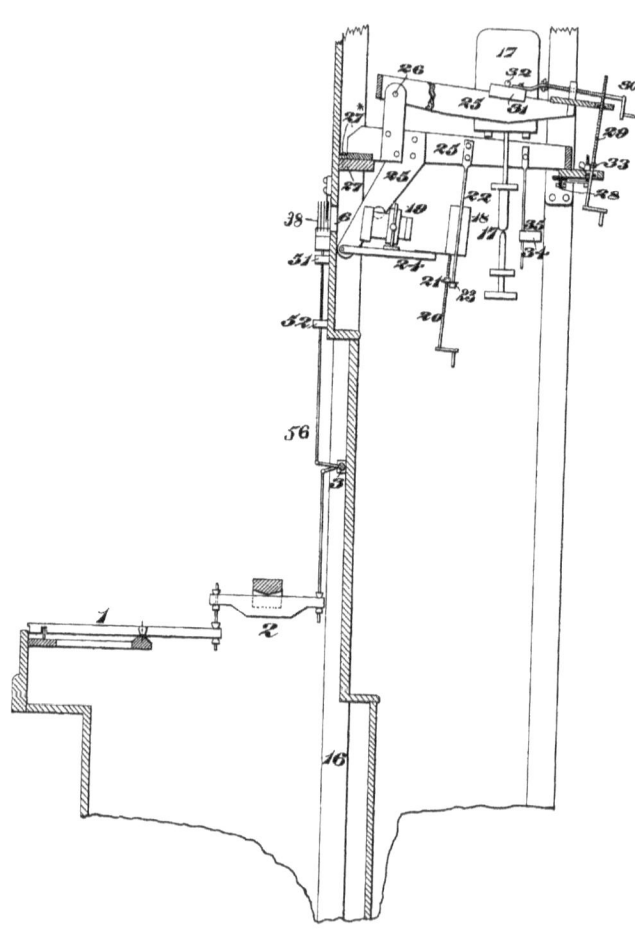

*Figure 3.*

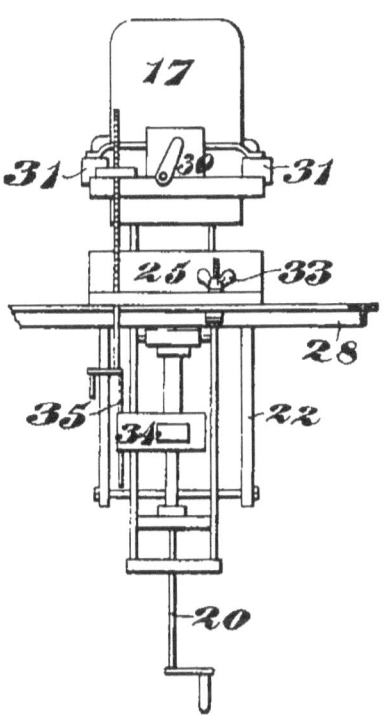

*Figure 4.*

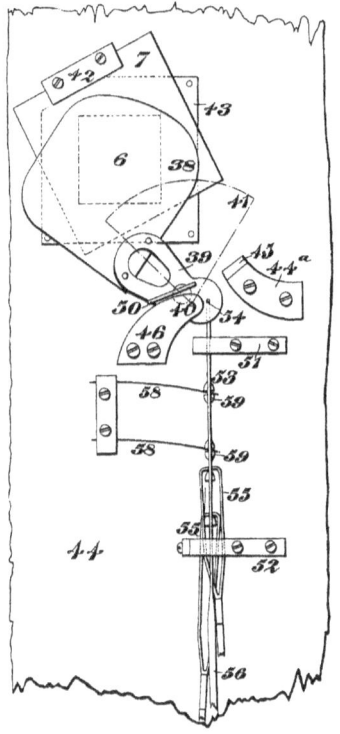

*Figure 5.*

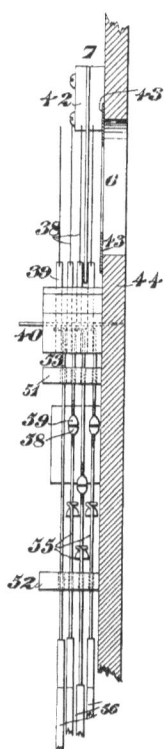

*Figure 6.*

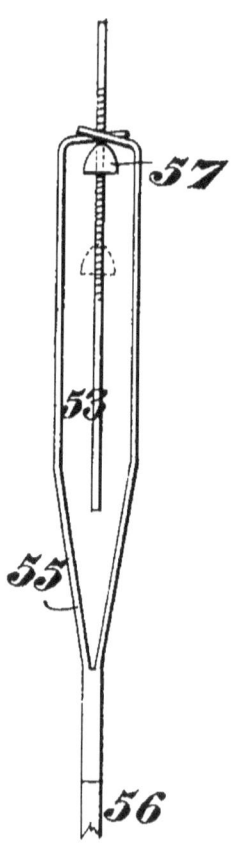

*Figure 7.*

*Figure 8.*

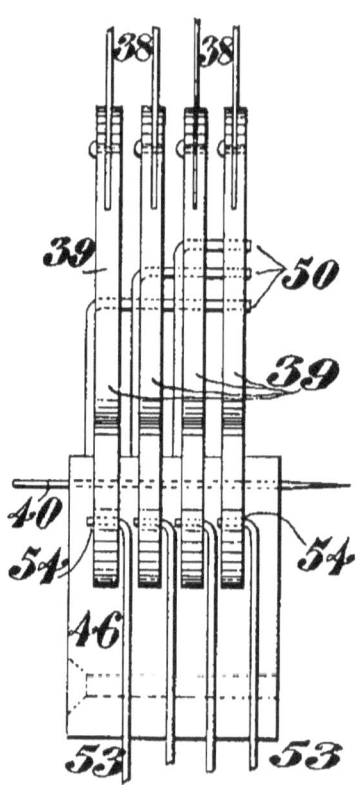

*Figure 9.*

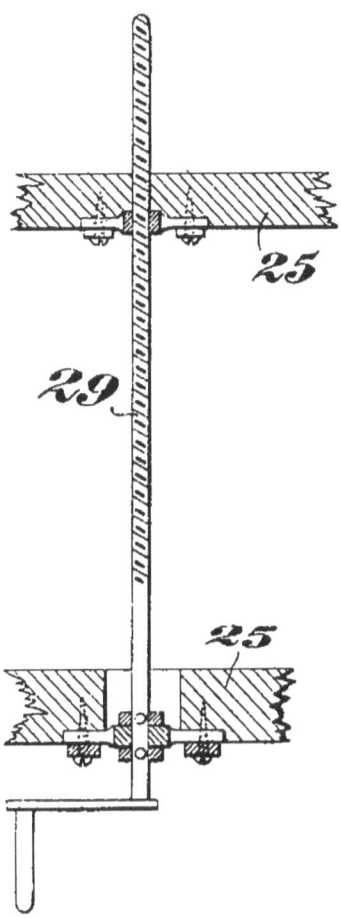

*Figure 10.*

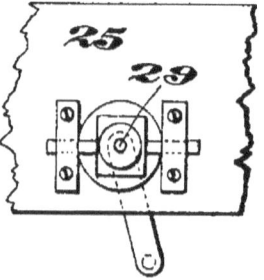

*Figure 11.*

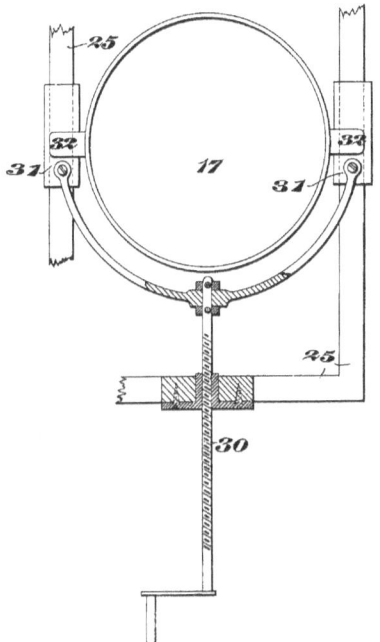

*Figure 12.*

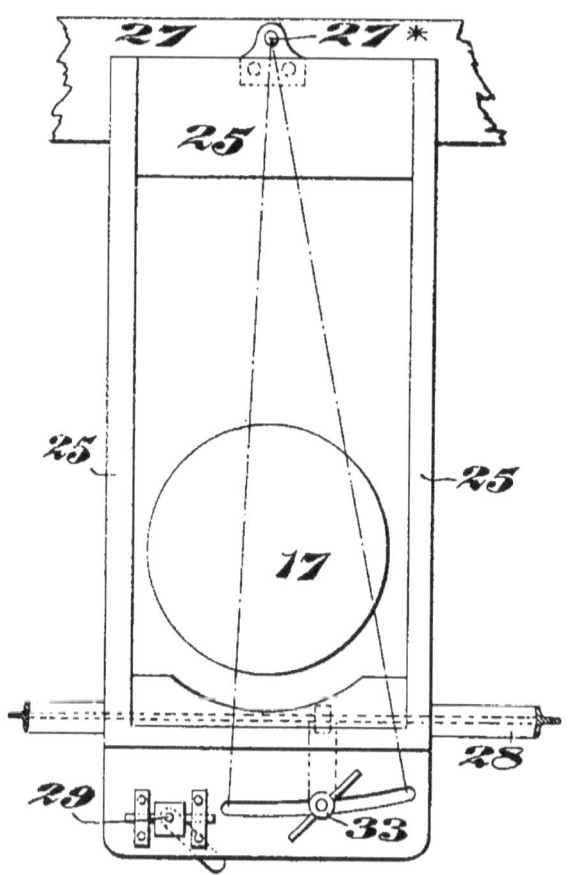

*Figure 13.*

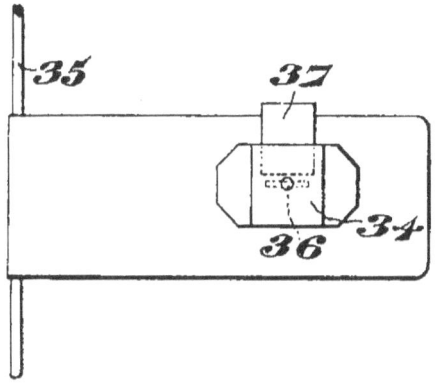

*Figure 14.*

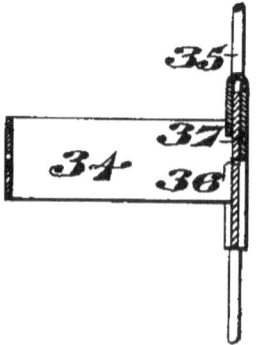

*Figure 15.*

# Colour-Music | 37

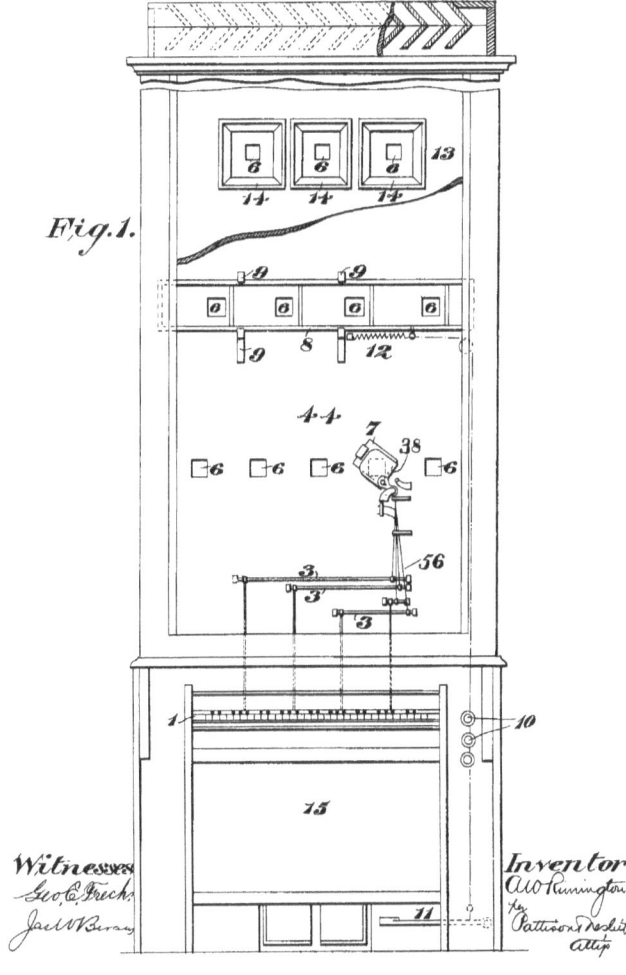

*Original patent illustration.*

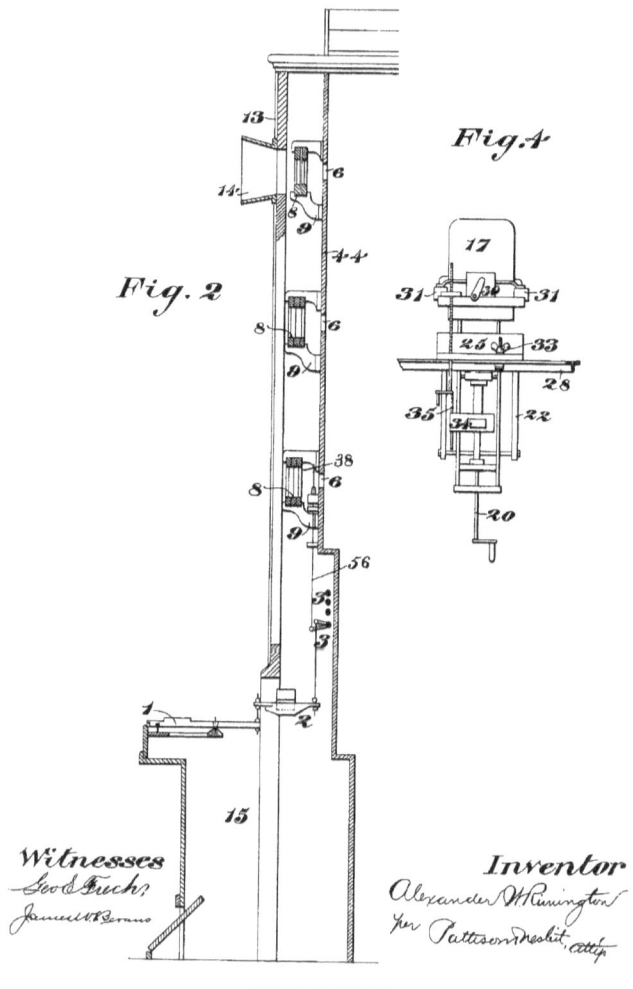

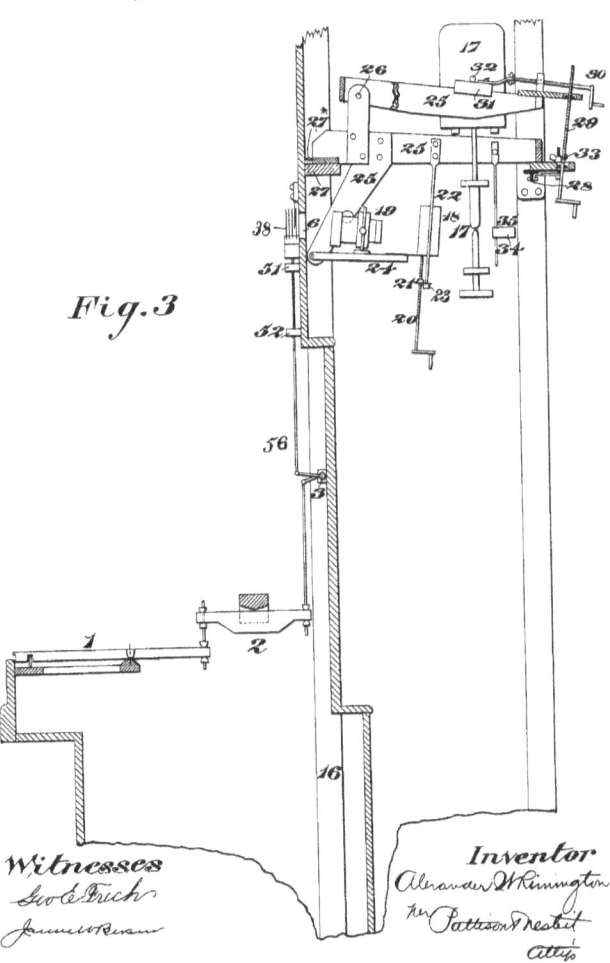

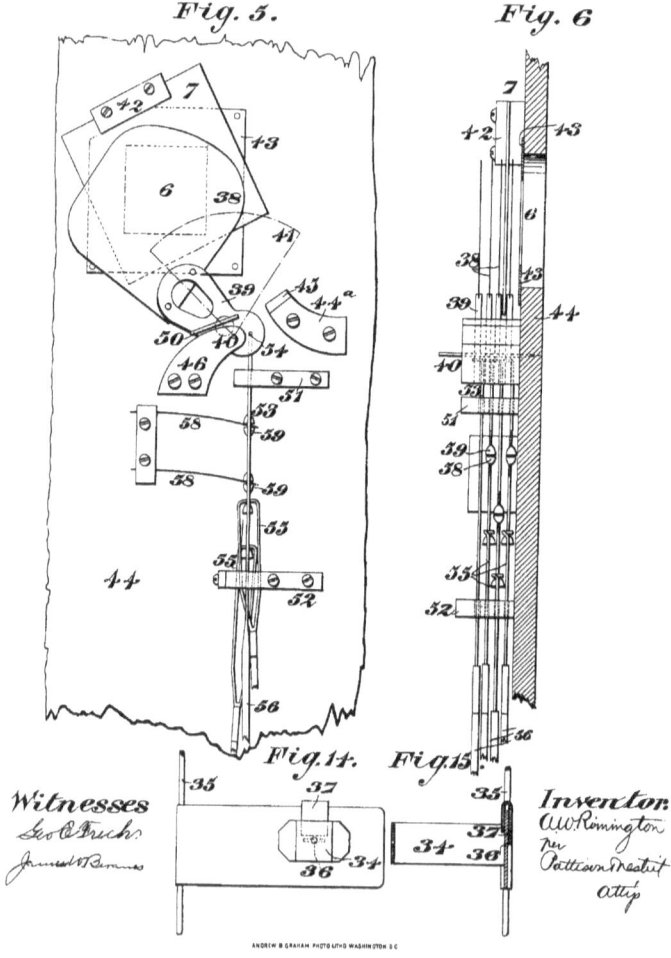

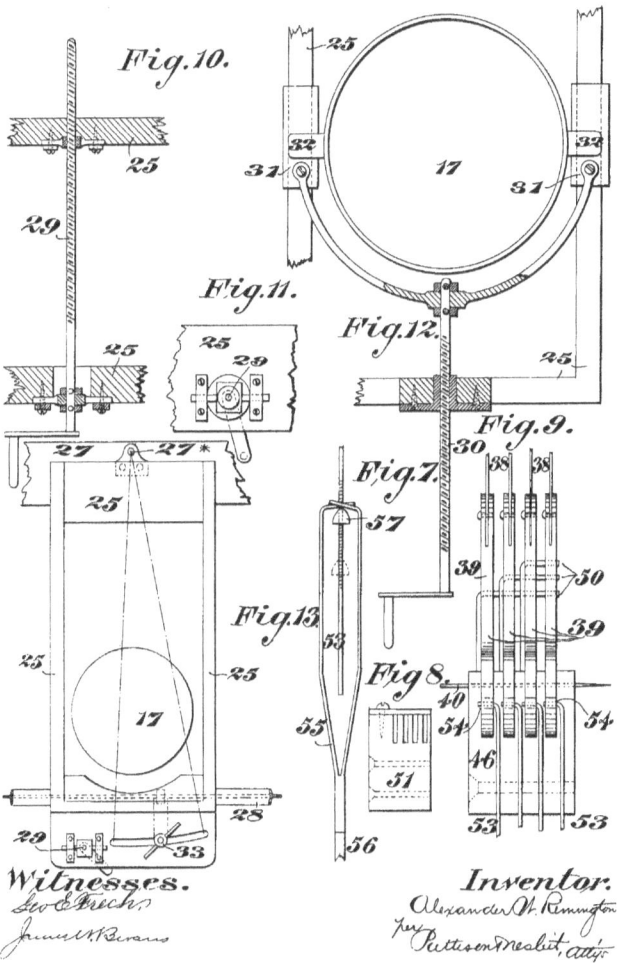

# A New Art: 'Colour-Music'

LADIES AND GENTLEMEN,
Perhaps as the instrument I am about to show you, and the art which it has rendered possible, are so entirely new, you will allow me to say a few words in explanation.

Very briefly, my aim has been to deal with Colour in a new way, and to place its production under as easy and complete control as the production of sound in Music.

Until now colour to a large extent in nature, and altogether in art, has been presented to us without mobility and almost invariably associated with form. Colour combined with form has constituted the whole colour art of the world.

In painting colour has been used only as one of the elements in a picture, although perhaps the greatest source of beauty. We have not yet had pictures in which there is neither form nor subject, but only pure colour. Even the most advanced impressionism has not carried us thus far. In decorative art colour has, broadly speaking, held the same position.

Moreover, to obtain particular tints of colour it has been necessary to mix them laboriously on the palette or in the dye-house. Art hitherto has not been able to compete in any sort of way with Nature in the mobility of her multitudinous and ever-varying combinations of colour.

There has, in fact, been no pure colour art dealing with colour alone, and trusting solely to all the subtle and marvelous changes and combinations of which colour is capable as the means of its expression.

The object of the present invention is to lay the first stone towards the building up of such an art in the future.

The chief problem, then, that the new art sets itself is to introduce mobility into colour, and with this changefulness, the three great influences of Time, Rhythm, and Combination, slow or rapid and varied. Colour thus is freed from the trammels of form, and dealt with for the sake of its own loveliness.

To turn to the practical side of the matter, *How has this been made possible?*

Many here present are men of great scientific eminence, and there are others again to whom the science of light and colour is familiar. To these I must apologize for touching upon a few simple facts, in order to make the matter clearer to those of my guests who do not possess this special knowledge.

Let me then begin by saying that to deal in this way with colour we must go to the source of all colour—namely, light. If we take a ray of white light, we have that which contains every colour in nature. Such a ray may be split up into all the colours which compose it, by being passed through a prism and spread out into what is known as the spectrum band; which I propose to show you in a moment. Any tint or shade of colour may be obtained by recombining in the required proportions the simple colours which you will see in this band.

Here is such a ray produced by the electric arc.

Pass it through a pair of prisms, and it is spread out into the spectrum band you see before you.

In the instrument I have invented, and which I propose to call the 'Colour-Organ,' I have taken a certain number of points, at carefully calculated intervals, along the whole length of this spectrum band, and have devised means for obtaining the colour at these points as accurately as possible, in much larger quantity, and in variable intensity. The colours thus selected have been placed under the control of a keyboard like that of a pianoforte.

I do not here propose to trouble you with a description of the rather delicate mechanism which intervenes between this keyboard and the diaphragms which filter out the colours required, and which has been a source of great difficulty in the construction of the instrument, but suffice it to say that, upon the depression of any note, the corresponding colour by these mechanical means is projected upon the great screen at the end of the hall. Thus each note of the keyboard has its own distinct and permanent colour corresponding to the proper interval on the spectrum band, just as each note of the pianoforte has its own distinct musical sound. The keyboard is, in fact, a large palette from which we can paint with instantaneous effect upon the screen the colours being at will combined into one chord, or compound tint, upon its surface.

I now come to an interesting side of the subject, which, however, may easily be misunderstood.

As I have said, this new art introduces three novel elements into the use of colour—viz. time, rhythm, and instantaneous combination.

It is evident these three elements are associated with one other art only—namely, music. Notes of music and notes of colour can in these respects be treated in exactly the same way. Hence the adoption of the term 'Colour-Music'—being impossible to find any other which would sufficiently describe the new art.

There are, however, other reasons for attempting to use colour as we use musical sounds, but about which there will be some divergence of opinion. I am, however, desirous of referring to them in a few words, because it was my great interest in this side of the question which first turned my thoughts to the study of the whole subject.

Taking the spectrum band as the basis of all colour, there are two remarkable points of resemblance between it and the musical octave, which have long been commented upon and discussed. The first of them is that the different colours of the one, and the different notes of the other are both due to various rates of vibration, acting on the eye or the ear. This is very simply and clearly put by Professor Schellen in his great work upon spectrum analysis. 'Different colours,' he says, 'are produced by the different degrees of rapidity with which the ether vibrations recur, just as the various notes in music depend upon the rapidity of the succession of vibrations of air.' In a word, 'colours are to the eye what musical tones are to the ear.'

At the end of this paper I have quoted a number of scientific opinions on this and other points, which I need not trouble you with now. I will therefore pass to the second and equally remarkable analogy between the octave of colour and the octave of sound.

If we measure the rate of vibration at the first visible point at the red end of the spectrum, we shall find it is approximately one-half what it is at the extreme violet end. Now in music, as we all know, this relationship is the same. If we take the first and last notes of an octave (by which I mean the twelfth) the latter has nearly double the number of air vibrations—and the first note of the new octave has exactly double. This, as we have seen, is the case also with the spectrum band so far as the one octave is concerned; the lowest red stands for the first note of the octave, and the highest violet for the twelfth or last note. Further than this, the blue end of the spectrum shows a tendency to a return to red in the violet, and the red end of the spectrum shows a similar tendency towards a reappearance of blue, in the fact that it passes from scarlet to carmine before it fades away, so that Sir John Herschel and others may have been right when they surmised that, if our eyes could see them, the colours of the visible spectrum would probably repeat themselves in successive octaves, in the great invisible portions beyond the red and the violet.

Starting from these remarkable physical analogies, I have divided the spectrum band into diatonic intervals or notes, on the same plan as that of the musical scale. These intervals I will now show you approximately, by drawing a black screen in front of the white one, with slits in it roughly corresponding to these carefully calculated intervals or notes of the colour octave. You will observe that these points are unequal in distance. This is because the rays of the spectrum are unequally retractable, but the colour notes are, as nearly as can be calculated, separated by equal intervals of vibration.

It will be a question of opinion, and of further experiment, whether the close physical analogy between the octaves of colour and sound has its physiological and Psychical counter-part. Perhaps our eyes, as a well-known musician has suggested to me, are not yet sufficiently educated to make us competent judges, but the new art is not dependent upon its demonstration.

As a working theory, the analogy has its uses, and for this reason I have constructed the new instrument upon it.

The possession of a keyboard similar to the musical one renders it possible to write colour compositions upon the same system of notation, and what for the present is important, to translate musical scores into colour, and make use of the beautiful rhythmical works already in existence for the interpretation of, and to help in the development of, the new art.

The middle **C** having usually been the note selected for fixing the pitch of a keyed instrument, it would seem natural to take it as the first point of contact between the two scales.

In thus translating sound music into colour music, I have found that it adds much to the enjoyment of the colour if the music is simultaneously rendered into sound, and it is curious to note how extremely sensitive the eye soon becomes to the least divergence of time or accent.

That colour, like sound, is capable of expressing artistic emotion there can, I think, be no question, but whether it expresses it in the same way as music is doubtful. It is, however, a somewhat strong argument in favour of the existence of the physiological and psychical analogy, that when we avail ourselves of the works of great musical composers for the interpretation of the new art, the results are vastly superior in variety, delicacy, and beauty of colour to those hitherto obtainable by other methods.

If this discovery be, as I claim, a *new* art, it is evident that the science of its interpretation still remains to be constructed. The principles which underlie its artistic and scientific application have still to be determined. Some investigation and experiments I have made, but time has been too short to allow of any definite results being arrived at. In the meantime till such research can be pursued, completed, and applied, there is an immense store of beauty in the musical works we already have.

But the question will be asked, *What are the uses of this new art?* In reply, I would venture to ask, *What are the uses of any art?*

Are they not to ennoble, to refine, to increase the pleasures and interests of life, to educate the special sense or senses to which they minister?

All these missions I venture to claim for the new art, although I admit to the full that time and experience alone can show the full range of its utility and possibilities.

The following brief, but remarkable and curiously prophetic expression of opinion, by a well-known author, confirms this view. It was written twenty years ago, but strange to say I had no knowledge of its existence until a few weeks since, and after my invention was completed. You will observe that it attacks the subject from the emotional side.

'The only possible rival to sound as a vehicle for pure emotion is colour, but up to the present time no art has been invented which stands in exactly the same relation to colour as music does to sound. No one who has ever attentively watched a sunset can fail to have noticed that colour, as well as sound, possesses all the five qualities which belong to emotion...

'Colour now stands in the same kind of relation to the painter's art as sound amongst the Greeks did to the art of the gymnast. But just as we speak of the classic age as a time long before the era of real music, so by and by posterity may allude to the present are as an age before the colour art was known; an age in which colour had not been developed into a thing of pure emotion, but simply used as an accessory for drawing as music was once to bodily exercise and rhythmic recitation.

'And here I will express my conviction that a colour art exactly analogous to the sound art of music is possible, and is amongst the arts which have to be traversed in the future, as sculpture, architecture, painting, and music have been in the past. Nor do I see why it should not equal any of these in the splendour of its results and variety of its applications. Had we but a system of colour notation which would as intensely and instantaneously connect itself with every possible tint, and possess the power of combining colours before the mind's eye as a page of music combines signs through the eye to the mind's ear; had we but instruments or some appropriate art mechanism for rendering such colour notation into real waves of colour before the bodily eye, we should then have actually realized a new art, the extent and grandeur of whose development it is simply impossible to estimate. But the colour art must first be constituted, its symbols and phraseology discovered, its instruments invented, and its composers born. Up to that time music will have no rival as an art-medium of emotion.'

I had hoped that the writer, Mr. Haweis, might have been present this evening, but he is unfortunately away from England.

I would ask you to make some allowances for the fact that to-night, for the first time, your eyes will be called upon to appreciate colour under new and unaccustomed conditions.

As only a well-trained ear can fully enjoy the subtleties of music composition, so with the eye generally in the new art is now called upon to appreciate the perhaps still greater subtleties of 'colour-music.' Therefore I think it is likely that to some (though I have not yet found any one) the new art will not appeal at all, and that others will have but a very partial enjoyment of its beauty. Still I believe that, as it educates the eye, there will be increasingly few to whom it is not a new and keen sort of pleasure, for it will, as has been predicted, sooner or later take its place with painting, music, architecture, or any other of the great arts.

There are some industrial uses to which the instrument might be applied to which I might refer did time permit; such, for instance, as a means of testing combinations of colour for decorative designs, etc.; but with these I will not trouble you further than to say that they open up an interesting field.

Form has ever been felt to lend an added charm to colour, and in the new art can be produced in many beautiful and interesting ways, introducing infinite variety and relation of colour.

The art in this connection is capable of great development. When, however, the element of what I call mobility is introduced into the production of colour as in the rendering of a piece of colour-music, it is a moot point if in any degree, or in what degree, the addition of form is to be desired.

During the experiments I have made it has been argued with some force that an undetecting eye has a sufficient task in its efforts to measure, compare, and appreciate mobile colour to a perfect performance of which it is more or less unequal, and that any additional element such as form, 'however beautiful in itself,' becomes distraction which hinders rather than aids its perceptions. The question of the introduction of form I do not pretend to determine, and I shall show colour-music with and without it.

Turning to another point, it will be apparent to all that the eye rapidly attains some education. I think you will all find that by the end of the evening you can appreciate intricate colour variations with far more pleasure than at the beginning.

I have said that to a large extent in nature colour is presented to us without mobility. Exceptions to this proposition will easily occur to us. Who has not experienced the profound emotion, partly joyous, partly melancholy, produced by the grand procession of glorious colour schemes presented by many a sunset? Here the changes are for the most part slow and solemn; red becomes orange, orange becomes gold, gold melts to delicate green and blue by almost imperceptible transmissions. Numberless combinations and proportions of every colour, in ever varying and progressing harmony march with slow and stately measure into the night.

Or again look at the restless sea, on a bright and boisterous day, with cloud squadrons charging overhead, how infinite and magical are the colour schemes presented to us! How glad and sparkling the emotions we experience! How different from those called forth by the pageant of the dying sun! Then our perception of beauty was tinged with a pathos that deepened as light yielded to darkness. Now we watch the quickest movement of a symphony where the variations are even too rapid for the eye to follow. No rest, no pause in the many changes of colour; the former is a procession, the latter a dance. Or again, combine the two; spread the rippling sea beneath the setting sun-how infinite in beauty and complexity becomes the very opera of colour! Did time allow, I might multiply examples. These colour compositions of nature are under the influence of form, gradation, and combination. No contrivance of earthly art can hope to rival in some directions these glorious manifestations of Nature.

But there are two qualities of mobility which I think have no influence over colour as presented to us in the natural world. I mean the influence of time in its musical, and rhythm in either its musical or poetic sense. In introducing these, the new art stands alone.

Such, briefly sketched, are the principles, aims, and methods of the new art. From sound man has developed music, that glorious art which has done an infinity to elevate the human race; but music is not with us always, or, at any rate, our dull ears perceive it not.

But how is it with colour—with light, for the terms are synonymous? Colour is with us all our waking hours—colour is of the essence of the beauty of this world. Surely, then, this all-pervading gift will lend itself to the high purpose of a great art whose influence shall be as deep, as far-reaching, as elevating as that of any of her sisters. I claim to have done no more than to give the first suggestions of its principles and possibilities. Only after the toil and travail of many minds, perhaps through many years, can we expect to see whither it will lead, or hope to approach its realization.

A. WALLACE RIMINGTON

# *Colour-Music*
## *The Art of Mobile Colour*

## AUTHOR'S PREFACE

THE interest aroused in the whole subject of Colour-Music seems to have become so widespread, and I have received so many inquiries with regard to it, that a short volume giving a brief description of the present position of the new art, and replying to some of the questions that are frequently asked about it, may perhaps not be unwelcome. Hitherto it has hardly seemed advisable to publish a book upon the subject, because fresh experimental work and frequent modifications of the instruments used in the production of Colour-Music have carried the art further and further into the field of the untried, but some statement of what has been and is being done should perhaps not be further delayed.

In writing these pages I have felt myself to be addressing two classes of readers, namely, those who know something of the art of

Mobile Colour, its past history, its hopes and its aims; and others who have never even heard of the subject. To the former, including, as it does, many of those who have followed and assisted in the experimental work carried out by me for a good many years past, I would take this opportunity of expressing my thanks for the keen interest they have shown in it, and the many excellent suggestions I have received from them; and, from the latter, I would ask for as open-minded a consideration of the subject as they can give me, more especially in view of the difficulty of placing it before them without being able, at the same time, to give practical demonstration of some of the points dealt with.

Upon a subject so new misconceptions are sure to arise again and again; but in the present statement of the case for Colour-Music, I have used my best endeavours to guard against them, and, discarding much more that might have been said from the artistic and technical standpoint, to write as clearly and simply as possible. I make no claim to absolute originality of conception with regard to the whole matter. Since I first took up the question of the need for, and possibility of, such an art as Colour-Music, it has come to my knowledge that even from very early times—perhaps prior to the Christian era—the possibility has been alluded to by various writers, and, in the sixteenth century, it took somewhat more tangible form in the mind of a Jesuit, Lewis Bertrand Castel. It was also referred to in an eloquent passage by the late Mr. R. H. Haweis, which I have quoted, with regretful memory of the author, in the Appendix, Mr. Haweis having afterwards become one of the warmest supporters of the forms given to the new art.

Starting from my original belief in the need for and the importance of such an art, which, when I first conceived of it, I supposed to have been hitherto unthought of, my personal part has been to devise instruments for bringing it into practical being and to develop, through a long series of experiments, some of the principles upon which Colour-Music compositions can be produced. This has demanded the expenditure of much time and thought upon the construction and reconstruction of successive instruments and experimental apparatus, and I have been tempted further and further in the direction of fresh modifications and improvements which have necessarily meant long delays. It took centuries to evolve an instrument like the pianoforte, and therefore no excuse need be made for the amount of time which it has required to produce the Colour-Organ and its allied instruments. Others will, I hope, in their turn, improve the forms and powers of these, and build upon the foundations I have laid. The development of Colour-Music is not a commercial undertaking, and I have no wish to exclude rivals, but rather to welcome them.

I should wish to express my indebtedness for valuable advice and assistance—or personal interest in the experimental work—received from the late Sir George Grove, Sir Wyke Bayliss, Capt. W. B. Marling, Mr. W. Basil Wilberforce, Mr. De Vere Barrow, Sir Hubert von Herkomer, and Professor Gregory, amongst many others; also to

Professor Silvanus Thompson and Dr. W. Brown, who have made suggestions as to the chapters of this book dealing respectively with the physical and psychological aspects of the subject. The notes contributed by the latter and by Sir Hubert von Herkomer will, I am sure, be read with special interest.

Whatever may be the divergencies of opinion as to how far the analogies between colour and sound extend, one thing at least is certain, namely, that Colour-Music opens up a new world of beauty and interest as yet, to a great extent, unexplored.

A. W. R.

# INTRODUCTORY NOTE
### BY
### SIR HUBERT VON HERKOMER, R.A., M.V.O.

THE analogy of music to colour has occupied many minds, but, so far as I know, no attempt has been made before to bring it within the scope of physical demonstration; therein lies the great value of Mr. Wallace Rimington's pioneer work in this fascinating field of thought. Although he calls his chief instrument, for the present, a "Colour-Organ," he does not propose to prove by means of it that certain waves of light have their exact parallel in certain waves of sound. He uses the musical keyboard merely as a convenience, and has, for the same purpose, split up the spectrum-band in accordance with the musical octave, but he does not necessarily base his general contentions upon any such division.

One of the instruments with a musical keyboard, which the author has designed, and by means of which he projects his colour on to a screen, can be either mute, or made to produce musical sounds simultaneously with the colour.

It has been denied by some that colour suggests musical sounds, and that musical sounds suggest colour. But it is safe to say that a psychological affinity *is felt* by artists and musicians between sound and colour, hence the use of common terms of expression between them. The painter speaks of a *note* in a painting, and a musician of a *tone picture*.

Amongst other claims put forward by the author is that of providing a new source of pleasure—a new art appealing to the mind and the senses—by means of colour alone, without form. But I see something besides all this in it—I see in it something "medicinal" for the painter, a "tonic" for the colour-sense of the artist, a suggester, a corrector, and a purifier.

Most painters in their career pass through several colour phases in their work that are difficult to account for. If there is such a thing as habits of thought (and we know there is), one may declare that there is such a thing as habits of colour in the painter. These habits of colouring will enable the spectator to spot a certain painter's work at a glance, and I cannot see that a painter's work can keep fresh and vigorous if he plays on one "note" of colour throughout his life.

Let me here say that the colour-sense is by far the most sensitive and delicate of all the faculties that go to the making of the artist's brain. The sense of *form* is far more robust and can bear severe handling. For instance, a painter can, by pegging away from a model, get his drawing right in the end, that faculty having something physical in it. Not so with colour; no pegging away can make colour good in a picture. Hence the painter surrounds himself with all manner of richly coloured rugs and hangings, in order to stimulate his sense of colour. I can, therefore, see clearly that an invaluable *tonic* could be given to the painter's colour-sense by means of Mr. Rimington's instrument for the production of mobile colour, even without necessarily laying stress on the affinity to music.

To sit at this instrument and improvise for half an hour whilst watching the ever-varying combinations of colour on the screen produced by the playing is not only an unspeakable delight, but of real health-giving effect on the sense of colour. How much more valuable as a stimulant is mobile colour than the fixed colours of a rug, which the eye gets accustomed to, and which thereby act no longer *as a tonic.*

Perhaps the author has in some measure overstated his case; but much allowance must be made for the enthusiasm of the pioneer. It may be questioned, for example, whether the contemplation of formless colour will call forth such great pleasure in the majority of people as the author believes; whether the close analogy of colour to music will hold good in as many respects as he also claims. In fact, many questions of doubt may arise in the reader's mind. But there is so much in the author's experiments, opening out such vistas of possibilities, that the whole matter should be carefully investigated before judgment is given. Without holding a brief for the author, I, for one, believe in the potentialities of his new departure.

An introduction such as this must necessarily be short, therefore I cannot enter into the thousand and one ramifications that surround this fascinating subject. But to sum up briefly, Mr. Rimington's mobile colour system seems to me a method to enable one to *see sound* and *hear colour*.

BUSHEY, HERTS,
*July*, 1911.

# NOTE

## UPON THE PSYCHOLOGICAL ASPECTS OF COLOUR-MUSIC

### By DR. W. BROWN

CONSIDERED from the points of view of the psycho-physics and psychology of visual and auditory sensations, a colour-music art seems full of promise. The analogies existing between these two realms of experience are numerous and, in many cases, very close—probably even closer than the majority of psychologists have hitherto been ready to admit. Too much stress should not be laid on the discrepancies between the quantitative stimulus-relations in the two cases, since the question is primarily a psychological one, and such discrepancies are not sufficiently pronounced to detract from the significance of analogies arrived at on purely psychological evidence. The emotional influences of colour, as those of sound, are obvious and beyond dispute, and the scheme of introducing rhythm —i.e. the time relation—into colour combinations opens up an entirely new field of investigation which psychologists will not be slow in exploring. Whatever the future of colour-music may be on the plane of æsthetic production and appreciation—and it seems to be exceedingly hopeful—the theory cannot fail to be of the greatest importance and productiveness for future research in the domain of the psychology of colour.

King's Coll., Lond.,<br>
July, 1911.

## CHAPTER I

### A MOBILE COLOUR ART

HITHERTO there has been no pure colour art, that is to say, no art dealing solely with colour for its own sake as music deals with sound.

Colour has held a secondary position in all the arts into which it enters, or has only been used jointly with other means of appealing to the senses or the emotions—and it has always been more or less associated with form. We are accustomed to see colour, if it is used at all, combined with form, and employed chiefly to emphasize and explain form, or to add interest and beauty to it, as, for instance, in painting and architecture, in decoration, and in other arts, and we can hardly realize its existence apart from form.

But though, in the case of sound, the great art of music has been created, no such art with colour for its main object has yet been built up. There is, however, no reason why this should continue to be so, or why a great colour art analogous to the art of music should not be developed.

Colour-Music, or the Art of Mobile Colour, is the art which fills this gap, and which after some years of the experimental stage now seems to call for further statement of its claims for consideration. That the development of a pure colour art of this kind has been so long delayed in the history of the world has probably been due, in great measure, to the fact that, although colour is capable of providing almost as much pleasure and interest as sound, and, as I shall hope to show, has quite as great, or even greater, power of appealing to the emotions, it is a far more difficult matter to devise an instrument suitable for the production of colour, and for placing it under the control of an executant, than to construct one for the production of musical sound.

It is, in fact, hard to imagine, and still more

so to design, any such colour instrument; whereas in the earliest periods a reed or a conch shell has been easily converted into a means of producing music, and almost every race has devised its own musical instruments at an early stage of its civilization.

The non-existence of a pure colour art has from time to time been more or less recognized and commented upon, but, owing probably to the difficulties just referred to, nothing has come of it.

Within the last twenty or thirty years, however, a desire to study and enjoy colour for its own sake has sprung up, and the art of painting has tended somewhat to devote itself to the production of pictures in which colour is the chief factor, and Whistler and others, with some appreciation of musical analogies, have gone as far as to call their pictorial works " harmonies" and " symphonies." But in most pictures colour has necessarily remained subservient, to some extent, to their subjects, and in any case a picture cannot give more than one colour scheme, or the solution of a very few problems in colour within the boundaries of its frame. Once painted, moreover, that scheme, harmony, symphony, or whatever the artist may call it, remains fixed and unaltered. At most it is a chord or two of colour, or a single colour-phrase, even though much may be sacrificed in expression of the subject of the picture, or even in truth to nature, to make that chord or phrase harmonious and interesting.

But the desire for a more developed colour art is at the root of these attempts to force painting to do almost more than it can legitimately or successfully attempt, and to sacrifice subject and much else to obtaining beautiful quality in colour, and an attractive colour scheme. Something, no doubt, has been gained, and the demand of the impressionist for interesting and beautiful colour at all costs is in great measure a just one; but the result of the attempt to make painting do what it is only possible for a mobile colour art to achieve has been to cause it to abandon many of its means of appealing to the artistic faculties which we cannot afford to lose, to narrow its scope, and weaken its position.

On the other hand, an art like that of colour music devoted solely to colour gives us what the finest impressionist or expressionist—even Turner and the greatest artists—can never give.

Experiment has moreover shown it to be certain that such an art has the power of appealing to the emotions to an extent which it is difficult for those to realize who have never seen it, and is capable of giving somewhat similar æsthetic and emotional enjoyment to that given by music, but appealing to and developing a different sense.

It may be said, with a show of reason, that pleasure and mental refreshment are not sufficient foundations for a new form of art; to which it may be replied that, even though the art of music rests mainly upon them, it is not contended that they are entirely so. The other practical advantages of a pure colour art will be dealt with later on.

Let us first see whether there is not only room for an art of this kind, but a great need for it, whether its absence under certain conditions of life does not account for some present-day tendencies towards artistic degeneration, and whether it is not worthy of our serious consideration as an influence in civilization. I propose also to show that it is not merely possible—a mere theoretical dream—but how, after some years of experiment, it has been brought into actual existence and is being further developed, and to give some description of the forms it has at present taken.

The instruments used and the results arrived at will also be described, various criticisms and objections will be replied to, and the future possibilities of the new art will be briefly foreshadowed.

## CHAPTER II

### THE USES OF COLOUR-MUSIC

LET us, in the first place, consider whether there is likely to be any real use for an art of the kind referred to, and what is the present position with regard to the general feeling for colour.

It may safely be said that hitherto, and especially in modern times, the colour sense has in a very large proportion of people been allowed to lie dormant, and their appreciation of colour in nature and art is extremely limited. This is probably due to there being so few means by which their attention can be directed to colour, apart from the interest it gives to the form of the objects around them. There is, in fact, a general insensitiveness to colour which we will consider more closely farther on.

Supposing an art with colour as its main object were in existence, its other advantages and uses, apart from any æsthetic pleasure and satisfaction it might give, are therefore not far to seek.

If any art is practised it tends to develop the faculties upon which it depends for its existence, and a pure colour art would thus help to restore and develop the colour sense. Experiment confirms this assertion.

If the colour sense were stimulated and developed, all those arts into which colour enters would benefit. If the painter had a more sensitive eye for colour, his pictures would be better ; the architect, with his colour faculty increased, would deal with colour to more artistic purpose in his buildings ; the craftsman would produce better colour patterns in his fabrics, his wall papers, his combinations of decorative tints, his enamels or his glass. If there were better and more harmonious colour in all the arts, the world would at least have gained something. Here, then, apart from its possible artistic and emotional value, *per se*, is a practical side to a pure colour art and an object for its existence.

It is probable, for various reasons, that at

the present time any widespread advance in the feeling for colour can only be arrived at by increased special cultivation of the colour faculty, and increased knowledge as to harmonies and contrasts and other qualities of colour; and this cultivation in its wider sense, it is contended, can best be developed by some form of mobile colour art, such, for instance, as that I have called, for want of a better term, "Colour-Music."

Apart from this, there is the increased need of such an art at the present time, because not only has there been neglect of the cultivation of the colour faculty, but because there has been an evident decay of it in most Western nations. Here and there is to be noted some slight revival of the feeling for colour, but in the main there has been a tendency for good colour to disappear from our surroundings, from costume, and from fabrics, from architecture, and from other decorative arts.

This can hardly be denied, and it would almost seem as though an advancing material civilization were inimical to colour, as Nordau and others have asserted. Be this as it may, amongst large sections of the population in many nations it is no exaggeration to say that any real feeling for colour has died out. As instances of this, take the working classes of most modern cities and even the peasantry of many European countries, amongst the majority of whom there is no evidence to be found of any real love of colour, and where enjoyment of it, except in its cruder forms, appears to have perished.

This is unquestionably a great loss, and we are only just beginning to realize its consequences and also how much the presence of good colour in our surroundings has to do with our enjoyment of life and even with our mental health. The whole subject of colour as a factor in our lives has been so neglected that its influences are not in the least realized, and it has come to be looked upon by the majority of people as concerning chiefly or solely the painter, the architect, or the decorator, and otherwise as of little importance. The extent to which colour in nature and in art, in its capacity for giving pleasure or pain, in its value for all kinds of delicate observations in science, in its artistic and emotional power, and, I might also say, its ethical influence, has been overlooked and neglected is almost beyond belief.

Perhaps this can scarcely be better shown by a single example than by the fact that the *Encyclopædia Britannica* contains no article upon colour, except from the purely optical and physical standpoint, or as a means of assisting protective devices in animals. There is hardly a word about its uses in art, or upon theories of its harmony and contrast, or those obscure questions of quality, texture, or luminosity, which are so interesting to the artist; still less anything as to the range of its action upon the mind and the emotional faculties.

It is with this emotional side of the subject that the new art of Colour-Music is chiefly concerned, and it is especially through such an art that it is possible to study the influence of colour upon our senses and upon our minds, and, through them, upon our lives.

## CHAPTER III

### RESEMBLANCES BETWEEN MUSIC AND MOBILE COLOUR

SOME of the contentions put forward on behalf of a mobile colour art will, of course, be questioned, if not altogether disputed by some people—especially by those to whom the subject is new, and, perhaps, not infrequently by those whose chief interests are centred in music or in science.

They will be further explained and defended as we proceed.

Meanwhile, for the sake of argument, let us assume that there is something to be said for them, and let us endeavour to make the whole question clearer by examining more carefully the points of resemblance between music and colour, and seeing what grounds there are for using the term "Colour-Music" in speaking of this new colour art.

First, let us ask ourselves, what is the place of music amongst the arts, and as an influence in modern civilization?

If we look at the matter dispassionately, I think we shall come to the conclusion that the whole use and influence of music rests upon its power of stimulating the emotional faculties. Whether the emotions aroused by it are identical with those of our ordinary life and experience, or whether, as some philosophic writers think, they are of a somewhat different and special kind, belonging, as it were, to a higher plane of feeling, matters little for the moment. The fact remains that music interests, refreshes, invigorates, saddens, or makes us glad through its action upon the emotional side of our nature, and is a language without words, through which the mind of the musician can speak to the mind of the hearer.

For instance, it is used almost universally to stimulate religious emotions and aspirations. It helps to put the mind into an attitude for receiving religious impressions and assimilating religious truths. As it fills the vaulted roof of the cathedral and echoes through its aisles, we feel the better able to understand the thoughts and realize the faith of the builders expressed in the very stones around us.

In the concert-room, is not the mental refreshment, the keen interest aroused, and the pleasure we receive mainly due to the emotional effect of music upon us? Our admiration for the technical dexterity of the executant, as also our interest in the personality of the composer's methods, counts for something; but music which consists only of dexterities, not based upon a theme acting upon the emotional imagination—music which expresses nothing beyond mechanical perfection—surely takes a very secondary place in our estimation.

Music, again, finds another use, as Plato remarked long ago, in stimulating the military spirit, in maintaining the soldier's courage and making him forget his exhaustion.

In a word, emotion, of one kind or another, is always called into play by music, whether it be of the kind which is aroused in the concert-room or the church, in the ballroom or on the battlefield.

The foundations of music, therefore, as

has been said, rest upon this capability of arousing emotional feeling, and it seems very remarkable that so great an art, and one which makes so wide an appeal to the human race, should have been thus based and built upon these subtle psychological sensations.

The action which colour has upon us in its harmonies and contrasts, its varying strength and delicacy, its power of giving joy or pain, is also, to a large extent, an emotional one ; and if a mobile colour art be attacked because it rests upon this appeal to emotion, music must be attacked on the same grounds.

If, on the other hand, we frankly admit, as I think we must, that emotional appeal is at the root of all art, then it may well be profitable to go on and examine the further points of resemblance between a mobile colour art and music.

## CHAPTER IV

### THE COLOUR SCALE AND MOBILE COLOUR

COLOUR, like music, is both precious for its own sake and as an educative influence. It also can stimulate the imagination and develop other mental faculties ; can give pleasure and refreshment to the mind, and increase the responsiveness of the sense to which it appeals.

Let us, then, begin to clear our path through the jungle of untried possibilities, which prevents our seeing clearly how to use these attributes of colour in a mobile colour art somewhat resembling music.

They are so striking and so significant that, in devising any form of such an art, we can hardly escape from them.

As most of us know, according to generally accepted scientific theory all colours are produced by varying frequencies of vibration of the ether acting upon the retina of the eye, and all musical sounds by varying frequencies of air vibration acting upon the ear. Both colour and sound, as we perceive them, are due to vibrations which stimulate the optic and aural nerves respectively.

This in itself is remarkable as showing the similarity of the action of sound and colour upon us, for within the variations of frequency of these two sets of vibrations are contained all, or nearly all, the impressions we receive of pleasure and pain, beauty or ugliness, interest or dullness, both in colour and sound.

If we go a little farther we shall find a second, and perhaps almost equally remarkable, point of resemblance, though I have no wish to lay undue weight upon it, and if it could be successfully disputed, it would not in the least weaken the position of colour-music as an independent art.

All music is built upon the octave. Western nations have mostly divided it into twelve intervals or notes, and Eastern ones into more ; but the octave is and must be the foundation of the division. And it is so because our ears demand it ; because we cannot escape from it ; and because for some reason of which we have no certain explanation it is in itself an inexorable psychological necessity. No sound without vibrations ; no musical notes without selection of certain definite rates of vibration carefully related to each other ; no such selection possible without reference to the octave. What, then, is the octave, looked at from the musical standpoint ?

Take any audible rate of regular air vibrations and you have a musical note. Consider it as the first note of your octave. Double the speed of its vibrations and you have the first note of the next octave above it.

Turning now from sound to colour, what do we find ?

If we experiment upon colour with suitable scientific instruments and split up colours of all kinds into their components, we arrive at the fact that all visible colours can be resolved into proportionate mixtures of those we see in the spectrum-band or the rainbow, both of which contain all the primary colours.

White light can be divided into its constituents, as we all know, by passing it through a prism. If we allow a ray of sunlight, or a beam of light obtained from an arc-lamp, to traverse a prism, after passing it through a lens and a narrow slit, and arrange the prism at a proper angle, we shall obtain a series of colours which, if received upon a white screen, spread themselves out into a long band, and range from a deep red to a very tender violet. This is the spectrum-band.

Below the red and beyond the violet are other rays, or other colours, which our eyes cannot see; but confining ourselves to those which are visible, and comparing this band of colours with the musical octave, we shall find at least one very remarkable point of resemblance.

If we get the physicist to measure the speed of the vibrations of the ether at the red and violet end of the band respectively, we shall find that, as in the case of the last note of the musical octave, the latter has approximately double the number of vibrations. The octave of colour is in fact practically complete, and a counterpart of the musical octave as regards the range of vibrations which produce it. It does not extend to the first note of the octave above it, but it constitutes one nearly complete octave in itself.

To make this quite clear let us place the two scales one above the other.[1]

Of course the selection of the note C as a starting-point of comparison is purely arbitrary. All that it is wished to show is that, recognizing the musical octave as the physiological basis of music, there is a corresponding octave of colour with its lowest and highest points also separated by a proportionate increase of speed of vibrations.

This is a very remarkable fact, and would seem to point to some common foundation or organic basis in nerve structure, or in mental constitution for receiving both colour and musical impressions. Its significance may, however, easily be exaggerated, and too much stress should not be laid upon it.

It is possible that it is a coincidence, and nothing more, but it suggests, as I have said, that there may be laws connected with the

[1] See Appendix.

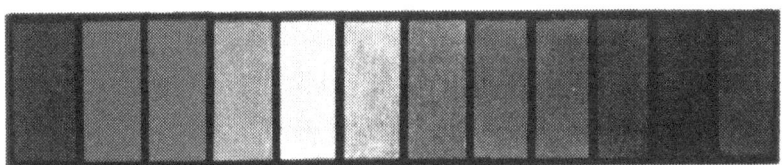

Chromatic scale in Music and Colour.
Shewing correspondence of intervals when C = lowest spectrum red.

nerve impulses of eye and ear, and their action upon the mind, which we do not yet understand.

There is, however, a remarkable and significant point to be noted which tends to carry the analogy a step farther.

Taking the last note of the colour-octave from the spectrum-band, namely, violet, if we examine it carefully we shall see that as it approaches the dark spaces beyond it into which our eyes cannot penetrate, it tends more and more towards becoming purplish before it finally fades into a dark neutral tint. In other words, purple being a mixture of blue and red, it has more and more red in its composition. This suggests as a possibility that if our eyes could see more of the dark rays falling on the screen beyond the blue and violet, we should again receive the impression of red. If so, this would be a repetition of similar notes in a succeeding octave as in music. Sir J. Herschel remarked upon this in the following passage: " I cannot persuade myself that they could fail to recognize a certain redness in the colour of the violet, which Newton appears to have had in view when he regarded the spectrum as a sort of octave of colour, tracing in the repetition of redness in the extreme refrangible rays the commencement of a higher octave too feeble to affect the sight in its inferior tones."

An examination of the red end of the spectrum also, I think, reveals a tendency towards carmine before it fades away into darkness, which means the presence of a small proportion of blue in the red, and perhaps suggests a return to the violet of an invisible octave.

It is of course evident that in the case of the musical scale there are many octaves, but in that of colour we have only one, and one which is not quite complete as to part of its last note. This is, however, from the mobile colour point of view, compensated for by the far greater variety of combinations possible in colour than in sound, and the immensely greater sensitiveness of the eye to minute differences of " pitch " as compared to the ear, as I shall show later.

This brings us to a further resemblance.

As with colour, so with sound ; there is a

long range of vibrations below and above the first and last visible colour and first and last audible note, of which we are unconscious.

The invisible rays beyond each end of the spectrum-band can be photographed and made evident in other ways, and it is extremely probable that various animals and insects are visually affected by them, though we are not consciously so. Similarly, there are many air vibrations which we cannot hear, but which other creatures are sensitive to, though to us they are beyond each end of the audible musical scale. In both cases it is only a limited range of vibrations that can act upon our senses, which have, as it were, selected this range for their own purposes.

The question now arises as to whether there are discords and harmonies in colour as in music, and what points, if any, of resemblance there are between the action of these respectively upon our senses. This is an important point, because if an art of mobile colour is to be developed and we are to obtain any assistance from the example of the methods of the older art of music, harmony and discord and intermediate stages between them must play a great part in its construction.

All musical compositions depend largely upon the approach to, or the divergence from, what is thoroughly pleasant, namely, harmony or concord, or what is thoroughly painful, namely discord, and even the lightest music is more or less dependent upon this undercurrent of pleasure and pain based upon concord and discord.

Turning from sound to colour, there can of course be no question as to the broad fact of the existence of discords and harmonies of great power and wide range. Everyone realizes this more or less. Most people are pleased by the decoration and furnishing of a room if it is harmonious, and displeased by a glaring discord in a picture or a wall-paper, a dress or an advertisement-board.

Those who have a highly developed colour faculty feel these discords acutely, and those whose colour sense is weak somewhat less, but few are quite unconscious of them.

To appreciate subtle harmonies in colour as in music requires a trained sense, and to reproduce or create any series of refined and beautiful harmonies in either requires an educated and sensitive eye and an artistic mind. In fact, we all admit the existence of discords in speaking of crude colours and vulgar contrasts, and there are certain juxtapositions of colours which almost everyone feels to be painful. And, in referring to contrast, it should, of course, be added that it plays so great a part in the relative pleasantness and unpleasantness of colours, that as soon as any individual colour is placed side by side with another its beauty is either diminished or increased, or altogether destroyed.

Here, then, we again have a characteristic of colour which is extremely like what we find in music, when the simultaneous sounding of two notes each pleasant in itself may produce a discord.

Elaborate experiments have been carried out in Austria and Germany with the object of finding a basis for determining upon scientific grounds which colours should be regarded as beautiful and which as ugly. It has been found that with single and isolated colours there is a certain unanimity of opinion as to the beauty of certain tints, amongst several hundred persons taken at random from all classes and submitted to the same tests ; and physiological theories have been put forward by Professor Exner and others to account for this. But he and other investigators all admit that the influence of contrast, both as to tint and as to intensity, overrides all these calculations when they are put into practice.

In other words, all decorative arrangements of colour are dependent for their effect and their beauty upon properly adjusted contrasts and harmonies as in music.

In the latter art, as just pointed out, if we sound a single note, beautiful in timbre and pure in quality, we can instantly make it intolerable by another, also beautiful and pure in itself but discordant when sounded at the same time. And exactly in the same way, a colour exquisite in itself can be made painful to the educated and sensitive eye by placing another beautiful but discordant colour side by side with it. Every artist learns this with the *a b c* of his professional work.

there is a certain unanimity of opinion as to the beauty of certain tints, amongst several hundred persons taken at random from all classes and submitted to the same tests ; and physiological theories have been put forward by Professor Exner and others to account for this. But he and other investigators all admit that the influence of contrast, both as to tint and as to intensity, overrides all these calculations when they are put into practice.

In other words, all decorative arrangements of colour are dependent for their effect and their beauty upon properly adjusted contrasts and harmonies as in music.

In the latter art, as just pointed out, if we sound a single note, beautiful in timbre and pure in quality, we can instantly make it intolerable by another, also beautiful and pure in itself but discordant when sounded at the same time. And exactly in the same way, a colour exquisite in itself can be made painful to the educated and sensitive eye by placing another beautiful but discordant colour side by side with it. Every artist learns this with the *a b c* of his professional work.

It cannot, further, for a moment be denied that the ranges of beautiful harmonies in colour, as in music, are almost infinite. Even if we take the harmonies producible by admixture of the various colours of the spectrum in one degree of depth or luminosity, millions of such harmonies are possible. And, when we consider that the eye is capable of appreciating a vast variety of degrees of luminosity of each colour, we see how difficult it is to assign any limits to harmonious sequences of colour ; and this applies of course also to discords and partial discords.

We have, therefore, in colour, as in music, both discord and harmony, wide in their scope and mutually dependent. We can in both produce series and sequences of harmonies differing in their degree of pleasantness. We can change them into discords and resolve them again into harmonies, we can, in fact, use colour as we use musical sounds, and we know that, although the physiological laws which govern the effects of both upon us may be obscure, they exist, and in some respects are common to eye and ear.

In music, after centuries of experiment, we have ascertained much more about them than we have as yet succeeded in doing in the case of colour, but the art of colour-music is now enabling us to pursue the subject much farther than has ever been possible before, as will be shown later on.

Passing on from this broad statement as to the general analogy, the next question may well be whether there is any close resemblance in detail between the musical scale and the spectrum-band in respect of harmony and discord—whether we can divide the range of visible colour into intervals like those of the notes of the octave, and whether, having done so, we shall find the same relative discords and harmonies.

There are great difficulties in making this comparison, as we shall see, but we may begin by pointing out one remarkable and perhaps significant resemblance.

If we strike the first note of the musical octave—say the middle C of the pianoforte, and also the last note, the seventh—we have a peculiarly disagreeable combination of sounds, a discord in the strongest sense of the word.

If we take a patch of red from the red end of the spectrum and place it side by side with a patch of blue-violet, we also have for most people a most unpleasant and crude contrast—a discord in colour for the educated eye—and if we combine the red and the blue, we obtain a compound colour which, by fairly general consent, is a disagreeable one—namely magenta.

This, again, seems to point to some underlying physiological law of sensation common to the organs of seeing and hearing, or to some laws governing the mental impressions received through them; but when we try to go farther we are met by various difficulties, some of them so considerable as to lead many to doubt whether there is any parallel here.

Let us go into these difficulties a little more carefully.

In the first place, as has already been said, the construction of the musical octave is somewhat arbitrary. An octave has been generally agreed upon as consisting of seven whole tones and five half-tones—seven white keys and five black keys on the pianoforte.[1]

All modern European music has been composed in conformity to this scale or to others very closely resembling it, but we must not forget that it is an arbitrary one. The Greeks had a different division in classic times, and some of the Oriental nations have another very divergent one to this day.

From time to time new and more accurately divided scales have also been introduced, but as they would have rendered obsolete all previously written music, none of them, so far, have found favour with the modern musical world. Amongst these may be mentioned the harmonic scale of Baillie-Hamilton.

If, then, we were to apply the ordinary division of tones to the colour-band, dividing it into similar intervals according to rates of vibration, we should be applying an arbitrarily constructed scale.

---

[1] See the diagrammatic scale by Professor Gregory on p. 122, and Note upon the defects of the diatonic scale in the Appendix.

We should have, moreover, to decide what musical note to take as the first note of our scale to correspond with the lowest tint of red of the spectrum-band.

Let us suppose that we take the middle C. We have then introduced two arbitrary conditions. First, the method of division of our octave; secondly, its starting-point.

In drawing any deductions as to the extent of the direct analogy between the two scales of sound and colour, we must bear this in mind and remember that it can scarcely be positively asserted that an analogy holds good or that it fails.

Further than this the colour sense has been so little educated as an æsthetic faculty as compared with the high cultivation of the musical one through past centuries that, although there is, perhaps, a general agreement as to certain pronounced discords, in colour—though even that is open to question —there is not the same general sensitiveness amongst most people as to lesser ones. Hence, although there may be a general agreement as to the discord between the juxtaposition of the colours at the beginning and end of the spectrum-band, there will be less unanimity as to whether intermediate combinations are discordant, even supposing we have divided our colour scale correctly and started it from the right point. Opinion as to what constitutes a discord in music is, moreover, undergoing a change and becoming less definite in its pronouncement, as is evidenced by some advanced modern music.

This portion of the general analogy is purely a question of opinion or of psychological investigation, and it is of little importance as affecting the main theory and practice of colour-music. In the earlier days of my experimental work, I was perhaps inclined to think it of more value as a working hypothesis in the construction of some of my instruments than I do at present, and there is, no doubt, a certain fascination about its mysterious possibilities ; but I cannot too clearly guard myself from being understood to lay any great stress upon the probability of its existence. Some physicists consider that there is no evidence to support the contention, others are in favour of it ; but it is really a question for the psychologist.

If it could be shown without possibility of dispute that similarly divided scales of colour and musical sounds have insufficient features in common to establish any emotional analogy whatever based upon numerical division, the general theory and the main advantages of colour-music as an art and as a mode of experimental research would remain unaffected, and the force of the chief arguments, which can be advanced in support of it as a separate and distinct art, would not be weakened in the least. The question of a possible analogy between the two scales is an interesting one, but how far it holds good is relatively not of very much importance.

# CHAPTER V

### POINTS OF ANALOGY BETWEEN SOUND AND COLOUR

WE have already seen that there are many strong points of resemblance between colour and music, and there are others which I shall touch upon in considering further questions connected with colour; but, as we have also seen, we must not attempt to insist upon the closeness of the analogy at all points, and for the present, until we have more facts to go upon, we must suspend our judgment as to the exact extent to which it holds good.

The points of resemblance we have examined thus far may be briefly restated thus:

1. Colour and musical sounds are both produced by vibrations acting upon the nerve terminations of the eye and ear respectively.

2. Both are limited to a certain range of

visible and audible vibrations, and there are certain numerical relationships in these which may or may not be of psychological significance.

3. Both are largely dependent for their common, mental, or psychological effect upon relative degrees of harmony and discord.

4. Combinations and sequences of notes or tints in both are capable of affecting us emotionally and giving us pleasure and pain.

5. Both are capable of adding interest to and deepening or lessening mental impressions received from other sources.

We have yet to consider amongst many others the following points:

(*a*) The musical resemblances arising when we make colour mobile and introduce the element of time into its production, or, in other words, when we make given colours and combinations of colours appear at will for a longer or shorter period.

(*b*) Resemblances in rhythmic compositions in music and colour.

(*c*) The conditions which arise when with the element of time we introduce repetition, gradation, and relatively quick or slow increases of strength and delicacy into colour.

(*d*) The emotional effects of mobile colour as a form of art upon us as compared with those of music.

In the first place—to return to a matter already briefly referred to—let us see how far it may help us if we use a similar scale to the musical one in designing an instrument by means of which we can produce colour somewhat in the same way as sound is produced for musical purposes.

Such an instrument should be able to produce all the simple colours, and, by combining them, almost any compound colours.

It should also enable us to place them side by side in larger or smaller quantities, or mingle them in one compound tint, and their production should as far as possible be entirely under the control of an executant as to their strength and delicacy, and the length of time they are allowed to appear upon the screen or other reflecting surface.

Several such instruments have been designed and constructed by the writer, and will be described more in detail farther on, but for the purpose of the argument let us merely assume the existence of such a means of producing colour.

Taking it for granted that we have provided suitable arrangements for producing delicate or strong passages of colour, corresponding to soft or loud passages in music, we shall find upon experiment that variations of strength in colour will produce the same kind of impression on the mind as in music, that delicate passages will have a quiet and peaceful effect, and strong and vivid ones will be more exciting.

We shall also find that we can take advantage of the influence of contrast as in music. Opposing colours can be used to make the action of each upon the eye and the mind more powerful, and partial combinations of divergent colours can be employed.

In music, a gradual or rapid increase in tone or strength—or vice versa—plays an important part in most compositions, and with our mobile colour instrument, or colour-organ, we can deal with colour in a similar way.

The faintest possible flush of colour can be made to swell into a full note or chord of great strength, and also to die away through a long succession of changes until it disappears.

A blaze of magnificent colour can be thrown upon the screen in a short sharp burst, or a few wandering notes can be made to flit across it, so delicate that we are hardly aware of their existence.

In the sister art, the gradual decrease of the intensity of musical notes has, as a rule, a pathetic effect upon the mind, whereas a rapidly increasing strength of tone has a joyful or stirring influence.

That the same thing applies to colour even in nature will be generally admitted.

The gradual dying away of colour in a sunset is usually more or less pathetic, and the increase of light and splendour in a sunrise has a certain joyfulness.

If we analyse our impressions, I think we shall find that this is not merely due to the disappearance and loss of the sun in the one instance and the hope of a bright day in the other, but to the lessening of beautiful colour and its final disappearance into a cold and unsatisfying grey or the gradual increase until it blends and merges into the full strength of daylight.

Experiments in mobile colour enable us to produce similar impressions.

Then, again, in dealing with colour, with the help of our colour instrument, we cannot avoid introducing the element of time.

If we strike a single note and produce a given colour upon the screen, the length of time that colour remains there before it is succeeded by another will correspond to the length of a note in music.

If we have a series of colour notes differing as to the length of time they appear, we also have something corresponding very closely to a musical phrase, and a good deal will depend upon the way in which we balance and combine the varying duration of each colour, just as in music.

To make the matter clearer, let us take a simple sequence of colours thrown upon the screen. We will say that such a phrase consists at its opening of a pale amethyst tint lasting for a quarter of a second, succeeded by a rose colour for half a second, after which the amethyst is repeated for an eighth and develops into a strong crimson for a whole second. Another short phrase may be stated thus, in diagrammatic form, and might be paraphrased by the series of musical notes placed under it.

It is quite clear, therefore, that here we have another point of resemblance between the foundations of an art in which musical sounds are used and one devoted to changeable colour under the control of an executant. Time—used in the musical sense—is more or less common to both.

This is worth noting because it is a key to some other facts about mobile colour.

It also leads us on to one of the other points of interest already referred to.

In music, as in poetry and architecture, there is always a tendency to rhythmical repetition. Passages are frequently repeated with a slight variation, and many compositions are ended with a restatement or *coda* of the leading motives which have been worked out in it.

# Colour-Music | 109

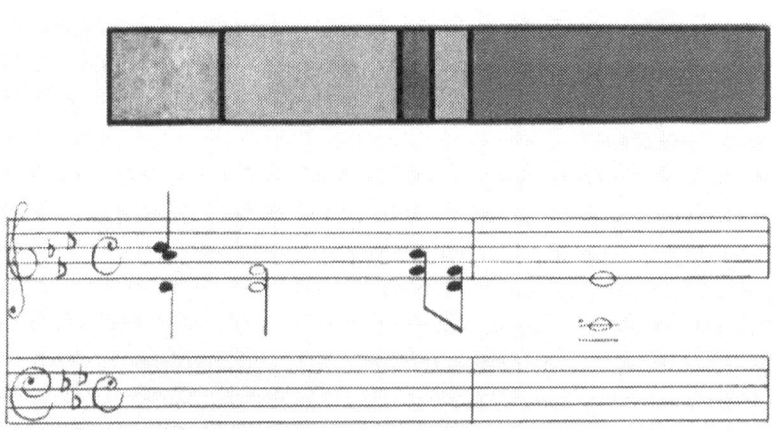

Diagram to illustrate introduction of the element of time into colour effects—the duration of the colour chords upon the screen corresponding to the musical notation.

In early poetry there are also tendencies towards repetition of ideas in echoing phrases, as, for instance, in the Psalms, and a rhyme is but a repetition of a somewhat similar sound at the end of another line.

In architecture repetition is still more formal and definite, arch repeats arch, and column echoes column, though varied perhaps in proportion or in the detail of its ornament.

We may also trace the same principle at work in the art of painting and in the pleasurable sensations we receive from nature. Intentional repetition of form with a slight alteration enters into the art of many of the great masters. It occurs again and again in the landscapes of Turner, especially in those wonderful colour dreams of his which are essentially rhythmic in their composition.

In nature it probably has much to do with our enjoyment of the inverted reflections upon the mirror-like surface of water. The beauty of the isolated stem of a silver birch, or the delicate lines of a group of reeds, is increased by their reflection in the pool of the moorland, and the campanili of Venice have an added charm when they are reversed in the wavering reflections of the lagoon.

In all these cases there is increased mental satisfaction derived from varied repetition, and we find, upon experiment, that this is also the case when we are using our mobile colour instruments, and endeavouring to produce beautiful colour sequences upon the screen. A passage of beautiful or striking colour seems to demand its echo.

Passing to the emotional effects of colour upon us, the important part that harmony and discord play in colour, as in music, has been already referred to. Much of the joy of life stands in direct relationship to the mysterious element of pain, and could not be fully felt without experience of discomfort or of suffering.

Even comedy borrows much of its joyfulness from our knowledge of tragedy, and in all great art there must be an echo of the pathetic as well as a suggestion of the pleasurable, or we feel that it is out of key with our experience of life and nature.

Here we find another peculiarity which is

common to both colour and music, and which is emphasized by a further mutual characteristic.

In literature the references to pain and to pleasure and to all the gradations of feeling and experience that lie between those two extremes are more or less definite, our interest is excited by descriptions of facts which suggest either the one or the other.

In music, however, the appeal to the emotions, except when music is allied with literature, as in an opera or a song, is essentially indefinite. With a musical composition —for instance, a Beethoven symphony—every hearer may well read a different meaning into its tender, its lively or its majestic passages. It would be difficult for a member of an audience to write a description of exactly the emotions or ideas suggested to him by a musical composition; and if two or more hearers did so, no two accounts would agree. A pastoral symphony may be in a certain sense descriptive, yet its descriptiveness is of a very indefinite kind.

In a musical work between its opening notes and its last chord there is a wide emotional field within which the imagination has freedom to wander at will. There are emotional suggestions, but no definite outlines —tragedy with no precise indications of its source—joy with no definite reasons assigned for it.

Part of the great value of music to us—certainly a great deal of the pleasure it gives —is closely connected with this indefinite quality, and its inexhaustible power in brightening, strengthening, and refining our lives, and in prompting our imaginations is largely dependent upon it.

A similar indefiniteness of action upon the mind and the emotions belongs also to colour, and experiment has shown that the art of mobile colour has for a considerable number of people, even in its present forms, the same kind of emotional and stimulative power that music possesses, though appealing to another sense.

*Exterior of a colour-organ.*

## CHAPTER VI

CONSTRUCTION OF COLOUR-ORGAN AND OTHER INSTRUMENTS

AS the qualities we have been examining are, to a great extent, common to both music and the new art, and as they are so numerous and carry us so far towards the same artistic aims and ideals, it would therefore seem reasonable to use musical precedents to some extent in laying the foundations of one form at least of colour-music.

Very possibly the buildings raised upon these foundations may, later on, be pulled down again and better ones erected in their places upon the solid concrete of newer experiences. Or perhaps, to use another figure, musical methods should be regarded as merely the scaffolding upon which the first arch is thrown across the chasm of the untried— but this matters little, they will have served their purpose and given us experience of how to build.

Almost all arts have been developed from others that preceded them, and we are beginning to see that what we supposed were absolutely new inventions in art are far fewer than we believed.

Greek architectural forms were developed from Egyptian and other Oriental styles; early Italian artists painted their Madonnas upon outlines which had come from Byzantium, and even the mediæval pointed arch may have been suggested by Arabic buildings.

We must walk before we can run, and as there is a sister art some few centuries older, perhaps it may be well for the composer in colour-music to accept her guidance to some extent in making his first steps.

Taking it for granted that something is to be gained by adopting musical methods for some forms of the new art, though they certainly will not be the only ones, let us see how this is possible.

In one of the principal instruments which

# Colour-Music | 117

*Part of the pneumatic "action" of a mobile colour instrument with keyboard.*

I have designed and constructed and used largely for experimental work—which will be referred to in future as the Colour-Organ—this has been done as follows:

    *a.* By dividing the spectrum-band similarly to the musical octave.

    *b.* By giving the colour-organ a keyboard like that of the organ or the pianoforte.

    *c.* By arranging for the general control of the whole keyboard by means of stops somewhat like those of the organ.

    *d.* By providing higher and lower octaves in the colour scale of relatively paler and deeper intensity, somewhat analogous, though not strictly corresponding to, the higher and lower octaves of the musical scale, though, of course, in the colour the wave-length remains the same.

It will be well to make this arrangement a little clearer by considering, first, the division of the colour-octave.

Taking the lower red *arbitrarily* as corresponding with the middle C, the octave is divided thus. (*See illustration.*)

This division was obtained in the following way.

The complete spectrum-band, greatly lengthened by sufficient distance, was thrown upon the screen by two bisulphide of carbon prisms—the source of white light being an unenclosed arc-lamp. An opaque diaphragm was then interposed close to the screen with an extremely narrow slit in it, and the fine slice of colour rays passing through it was made to correspond in position on the spectrum-band and approximately as to its rate of vibration to the notes of the musical scale in their relative intervals.

The narrow ribbon of colour, thus cut off from the spectrum-band, was then accurately matched and apparatus designed for producing it in larger quantity in the colour-organ and placing it under the control of the corresponding musical note upon its keyboard. The keys of the colour-organ were then connected with suitable mechanism for allowing these several colours to appear on the screen

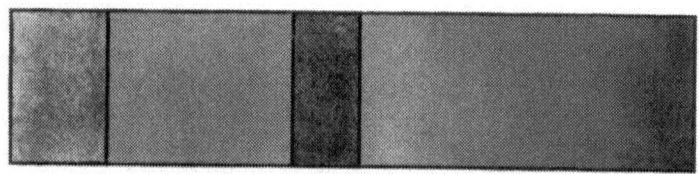

Illustrating a colour phrase, in which the fourth note is gradually increased in strength by the swell pedal of the colour organ.

as soon as the keys are depressed. The designing of this mechanism has been one of the great difficulties in the construction of the various instruments, as it was, of course, absolutely necessary that it should be responsive to the slightest touch upon the keys, and yet had to be far more elaborate than the action of a pianoforte.

A swell pedal was also provided, and if moved in one direction the brilliancy and intensity of the colour is increased throughout the whole of the length of the scale, if in the other, the colour effect is made more tender. Another stop enables either softened or "staccato" productions of the colour upon the screen to be given.

It is, of course, quite clear that, in order to use an instrument provided with a keyboard like that just described, it is necessary to devise some method of musical notation. Any absolutely new method would bring with it various difficulties, the foremost among them being the necessity for the executant to learn the new method, and for any composer in mobile colour also to be familiar with it. It would seem, therefore, that there is a good deal to be said for the adoption of a method which is already in use. This decided the author to employ the ordinary musical system—at any rate for all the preliminary experiments carried out by him—and it was soon found to be so convenient as not to make it worth while to abandon it in the later ones.

The keyboard of the colour-organ has therefore been arranged precisely in the same way as that of an organ or a piano; and, as has already been stated, the spectrum-band has been divided up into similar intervals.

This division of the intervals, or notes, corresponding to those of the musical scale, is not quite as simple as it would first appear to be, because of the fact that the rate of dispersion at one end of the spectrum-band is considerably greater than at the other. At the red end, where the dispersion is greatest, the spaces between the points from which the colour is obtained have to be greater in order to provide for the slower increase in rate of vibration, and at the violet end they are consequently closer together. This, however, is

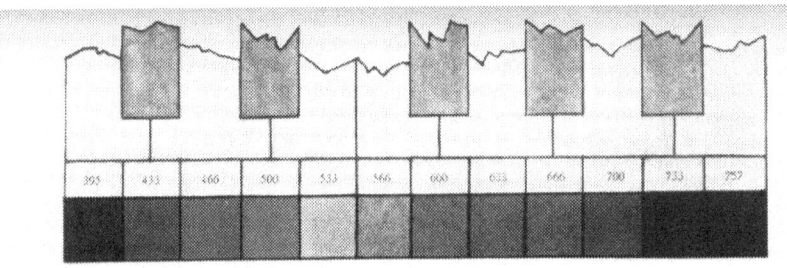

To shew normal division of colour scale upon keyboard of colour organ, colour musical methods of execution are employed. The figures in the spaces above the colours give the approximate frequencies of aether vibration in millions of millions per second. The colours cannot be accurately given in pigments, and of course do not correspond more than roughly to those produced by the instrument.

merely a matter of careful adjustment, as the increase progresses regularly upon a definite formula as in the case of a mathematical curve; and let it be again clearly understood that the division of the scale is merely a secondary matter and that other colour scales might perhaps be used with great advantage.

The method of musical notation being adopted as to the treble and bass clefs, time values of notes, etc., the ordinary musical directions such as *diminuendo, crescendo, allegro,* etc., can, of course, be used, and it becomes relatively easy for the executant to use the ordinary form of colour-organ.

Later on it was found convenient to have an alternative arrangement under which the spectrum-band can be spread over the whole of the five or six octaves of the keyboard. By the use of a pneumatic device, the simple withdrawal of a stop has the effect of doing this. A musical system of notation can still be employed, but when this stop is in use, of course, any direct translation of a musical composition is impossible, and a score written with the intention of using this arrangement of the keyboard would appear to the ordinary musician to be quite chaotic. Its chief advantage is to make extemporization in colour easier, and no more need be said for the present about its other uses.

Leaving the musical method of notation aside, we come to another mode of placing the colour effects under the control of the performer, to which some reference has already been made. It is that of using the three primary colours only, and combining them in various degrees of relative strength upon the screen. Under this arrangement each of the three colours can be projected in varying degrees of strength ranging from full power up to white light. Each colour is under the control of a lever, to which is attached an index showing the executant the strength of the colour he is using. The needle of this index passes along a curved scale, upon which figures or letters can be placed at intervals. Two of the levers are moved by the right and left hands of the executant, and the third by the foot. The whole arrangement places the performer more in the position of the violinist

*Levers of a three-colour instrument used conjointly with keyboard colour-organ.*

who has to find his note upon the string, than in that of the pianist who has each note definitely settled for him by the keyboard. The great advantage of this three-colour system is that almost infinite gradation as to intensity, and some approach to infinity as to variety of tint, can be obtained by its means; but, except for extemporization, it is, strange to say, much more difficult to use than the colour-organ of the keyboard type. A composition in colour can be written for it, either upon the musical method or in various other ways.

In using any but the musical method, however, the difficulty of easily expressing the duration of a note has to be overcome, or showing whether it is long or short, or accentuated, and so forth. An example is given below of the method of notation employed.

Each space represents a given note as indicated by its number on the index scale, and the length of the space determines the relative length of the note in the bar. The letters R. Y. and B. are the initials of the primaries.

To make the matter clearer by recapitulation :

When using the keyboard colour-organ, whenever a note is depressed its corresponding colour appears upon the screen, and if a chord is struck, combined colours also make their appearance. It will easily be understood that although the intervals taken along the length of the spectrum-band—to give its division into the octave of tones and semitones—are small, as in the case of the pianoforte or organ, there are spaces of colour between these intervals. The keyboard form of instrument cannot therefore provide quite the whole range of colours which appear in nature, although the combinations which are placed at our command are almost limitless.

There is one point of interest which may be mentioned here. When we are using coloured light instead of pigment, although the effects produced are much more beautiful than those obtainable with pigments, it does not seem so easy to obtain some of the grey tints with which suitable pigments will provide us. Greyness is, however, a relative term. In

# Colour-Music | 129

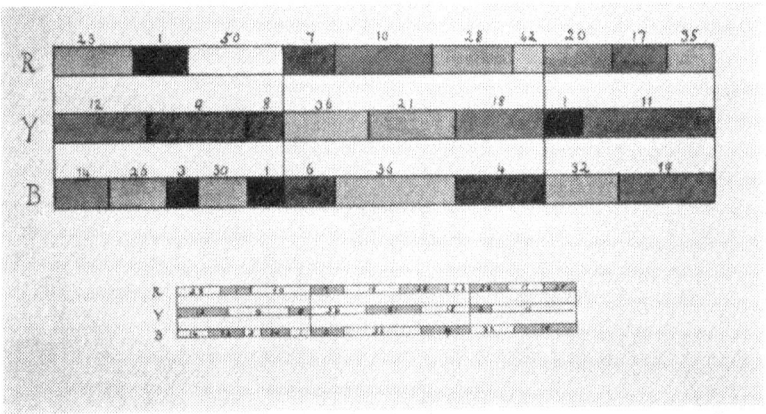

SYSTEM OF NOTATION FOR THREE-COLOUR INSTRUMENT.

The figures give the required position of the lever for each colour upon its scale, the tint within the space below it indicating approximately the strength of the colour. The length of the space gives duration of the note. Three bars of different time are given.
The lower illustration shows a smaller size of the musical staff in which the depth of the colour is not indicated.

the case of pigments a mixture of the three primaries in varying proportions tends to produce black or grey; but in the case of light, this mixture tends towards the production of whiteness. With paints or pigments, therefore, the mixture of many colours produces blackness or duskiness of the resultant tints; whereas, with the colour-organ, the more colours upon the screen the greater the approximation to white light. In using pigments, therefore, greyness is produced by a lowering of the luminosity; while with mobile colour instruments, on the other hand, it is due to increased luminosity. In both cases we have to compare grey or relative greyness with its surroundings, and with mobile colour the sensation of greyness is largely dependent upon the contrast between the colour upon the screen and the whiteness and strength of the two bands of light upon each side of it, which serve as standards for the eye to measure by, the other uses of which will be explained later on.

Although the present forms of colour-music instruments have cost me a large amount of time and thought and are the outcome of many modifications and experiments, there is still room for improvement in many respects, and I hope to carry out some of these improvements in the future or to be the means of suggesting them to those who may follow me in the pursuit of the subject.

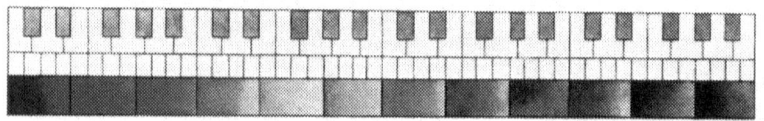

To shew division of colour scale when the spectrum is extended over the whole length of the key-board of the colour organ by spectrum stop.

## CHAPTER VII

### EFFECTS PRODUCED BY COLOUR-MUSIC

COLOUR and sound cannot, of course, be adequately described in words, nevertheless at this stage it may be as well to attempt to give some idea of the kind of effects produced by the colour-organ.

Imagine a darkened concert-room. At one end there is a large screen of white drapery in folds surrounded with black and framed by two bands of pure white light. Upon this we will suppose, as an example of a simple colour composition, that there appears the faintest possible flush of rose colour, which very gradually fades away while we are enjoying its purity and subtlety of tint, and we return to darkness. Then, with an interval, it is repeated in three successive phases, the last of which is stronger and more prolonged.

While it is still lingering upon the screen a rapid series of touches of pale lavender notes of colour begin to flit across it, gradually strengthening into deep violet. This, again becomes shot with amethyst, and afterwards, changing gradually into a broken tint of ruby, gives a return to the warmer tones of the opening passage.

A delicate primrose now appears, and with little runs and flushes of pulsation leads through several passages of indescribable cinnamon colour to deep topaz. Then suddenly interweavings of strange green and peacock-blue, with now and then a touch of pure white, make us seem to feel the tremulousness of the Mediterranean on a breezy day, and as the colour deepens there are harmonies of violet and blue-green which recall its waves under a Tramontana sky. More and more powerful they grow, and the eye revels in the depth and magnificence of the colour as the executant strikes chord after chord amongst the bass notes of the instrument.

Then suddenly the screen is again dark, and there is only a rhythmic and echoing beat of the dying colour from time to time upon it. At last this disappears also, and there is another silent pause, then one hesitating tint of faded rose as at the opening of the composition.

Upon this follows a stronger return of the colour, and as the screen once more begins to glow with note after note of red and scarlet, we are prepared for the rapid crescendo which finally leads up to a series of staccato and forte chords of pure crimson which almost startle us with the force of their colour before they die away into blackness.

This is an extremely simple example, but it may suffice to show the kind of effect produced by an unadorned form of mobile colour not accompanied by music.

Let us now try to obtain some idea of a colour-music composition associated with music. It was found after the first experiments that the beauty of colour compositions could be felt and appreciated without any musical accompaniment, but that, in some cases, it added greatly to their interest.

We will suppose for the moment an orchestral composition as being accompanied by colour. Let us assume that the composition opens with a Wagnerian trumpet-blast. The screen is at the same moment flooded by an intense orange which palpitates with the harmonic colours corresponding to a subordinate passage upon some of the other orchestral instruments. The blast ceases, there is a faint echo of it upon the violins while the screen pulsates with pale lemon and saffron, hardly discernible. Again comes the blare of the trumpets, and once more the screen flames with orange modulations.

This is the opening, let us say, of a passage of pathetic character in which accidentals often intervene and the key tends to become minor. The colour scheme, without being a direct translation, sympathizes with this—it is low in tone and shows slight discords, and then gradually in consonance with the sound-music develops a more joyous character. At last a modified form of the opening phrase is again reached both in sound and colour. This leads to fresh departures, and so the dual composition proceeds.

It might be tedious to describe it further, but this may suffice to give an idea of one kind of partnership which can be established between colour and sound.

So far, however, we have only considered the simple admixture of varying colour upon the screen by means of the first form of the colour-organ. This does not, however, by any means exhaust the resources of the instrument or the possibilities opened up by mobile colour. A few instances may be given of other ways in which the actual colour effects can be produced.

Let us imagine a low-toned tint upon the screen. Upon this is thrown a single spot of some other colour. That spot can be kept stationary or it can be made to move. It can be equal in intensity or can have a focussing point of brilliancy within it. If it moves it can be made to move rapidly or slowly, and if it moves very rapidly it will produce the effect upon the eye of a line or a pattern.[1]

[1] Professors Ayrton and Perry made some interesting experiments with a single spot of colour thrown upon the white ground of a screen and made to move rhythmically, some years ago in Japan. I was informed of this after some of my first colour-music experiments had been made public, and a further reference to the subject will be found in Chapter XIII.

Other spots may be added to it, also stationary, or in slow or rapid movement, and if in movement these movements may be in some sort of harmony or inter-relation.

Again reverting to our simple tint of colour upon the screen, we may imagine a second colour being thrown upon it and a net or reticulated diaphragm interposed in the path of the rays. The result will be that a portion of the second colour will be cut off by the solid parts of the net or diaphragm, and an interweaving of two colours, partly mingled and partly separated, will appear. If a third set of rays of different colours be projected upon it at the same time from another angle, there will, of course, be a mingling of three separate colours.

This on a large scale is very much what happens when the three primary colours are mingled in microscopically small dots by the three-colour printing process, but there is this important difference that each of two, three, or more interwoven colours can be instantaneously altered by the executant seated at the keyboard.

*Part of the "action" of a keyboard colour-organ, with colour-producing diaphragms removed.*

In this way results can be obtained of very great beauty, comparable to the interweavings of colour produced by a limpid sea reflecting a sunset.

In cold print all this sounds mere assertion, but I can only ask the reader to believe that the colour actually produced is far more beautiful than can be imagined or described.

The screen itself may also take various forms in order to resolve and break up the colours. I have experimented with various substances and materials, with opaque white drapery, combined with gauze veils at various distances, and other arrangements, in order to produce different effects. If it is wished still further to elaborate the complexity of the colour, the diaphragms can be made to move, and very remarkable results are produced by these movements. Some idea may be formed of them by imagining the delicate markings upon a shell to be seen in process of rapid formation and disappearance, by the movements of currents and eddies upon the surface of running water, and to some extent by the changing forms of a fleecy sky.

Advancing further in the direction of colour effects with a certain amount of form in them, it may be interesting to refer to another series of experiments which I have carried out.

It occurred to me that it might be interesting to substitute what are known as the "Watts-Hughes" sound-forms for the diaphragms above referred to, or to project the "Watts-Hughes" forms upon the screen in simple black and white at the same time as the colour tints. These sound forms are produced by causing musical notes to act upon films of liquid water-colour spread upon glass plates. When a musical note, or a series of musical notes, is played by a rather loud-sounding musical instrument, or sung by the human voice through a suitable trumpet placed close to one of these liquid films, the colour arranges itself in strange and decorative patterns upon the glass. The effects obtained upon the screen by interposing these plates are beautiful, but it would seem difficult to make use of them in writing a colour composition, though perhaps further experiment may show this to be possible.

*Portion of a three-colour instrument.*

Any method of introducing form into the colour upon the screen should be under the control of the executant, and the forms above mentioned being produced separately, cannot of course be under his control. They are only referred to because the results obtained have been remarkable and suggestive. The best method which I have devised of using them experimentally is to throw them faintly on the screen with pure white light, the colour being super-imposed upon them while in movement. This movement is given by a specially designed apparatus.

There are various other ways of modifying the colour effects upon the screen, which may perhaps some day be employed in orchestral compositions, but for the present it would seem preferable to adhere to the simpler methods of direct projection and admixture of colour, with but occasional use of form.

Some reference has been made to modifications of the screen, i.e. the reflecting surface upon which the colour is received.

The simplest form of screen is a plain flat surface of white, like that used for a projection

*Simple form of screen as used in the author's studio.*

lantern—but many advantages are obtained by varying this.

If the white drapery is hung in folds instead of being tightly stretched, the effects of colour upon it are more interesting because they have more " quality " in them; and substances with a certain amount of texture, like white velvet, are better than absolutely smooth ones. The screen may also be modified by layers of white cords at a little distance from it, hung vertically, and this gives a very remarkable resolution of the compound tints. There are other modifications about which nothing further need now be said.

Thus far we have considered the production of colour-music by one, or at most two executants, but great variety and splendour of effects could be obtained by the use of several mobile colour-instruments used simultaneously.

This side of the subject the writer has not followed very far, but it is evident that the field for experiment is large. Electricity makes the production and control of colour far easier than it has ever been before, and other supplementary forms of colour-instrument in which the colour is also evolved and controlled by electricity might be devised.

As a partial explanation of the great beauty of the colour obtained upon the screen, it must be remembered that all the colours visible upon it are produced by the admixture of coloured light and not of pigments. In colour-music therefore, as already pointed out, the greater the number of colours combined upon the screen the greater the tendency, roughly speaking, towards increased luminosity. This partly accounts for the extreme purity and beauty of the colour when properly combined upon the screen. Successive contrast—that is, contrasts of colours following each other, but not presented to the eye at the same moment—probably also has much to do with this exceptional beauty. Simultaneous contrast also exists when a colour-chord is broken up into its constituents by the diaphragms, or by the surface of the screen. So that in colour-music we have two kinds of contrast acting upon us, whereas in painting there is but one.

Another fact that strikes most of those who

see mobile colour effects for the first time, is that they are introduced to a number of colours which they have never seen before and to which they can give no definite names. The colour-organ is, in fact, an easy means of producing those ranges of colour which it is difficult or impossible to obtain by means of paints, dyes, or other pigments, and which are rare in nature or in other forms of art.

As already mentioned, the chief difficulty in appreciating colour-music at the outset lies in being unable to appreciate rapid changes of colour upon the screen. Some persons do not feel this difficulty at all, whilst with others it only disappears after some weeks of training, but as it disappears the desire for increased rapidity of change steadily grows. At first the succession of chords can hardly be slow enough to give satisfaction, while later on and after more experience the contrasting effect of extremely rapid passages is eagerly demanded by the eye and by the mind. This is interesting as showing the educative effect of colour-music upon the powers of the eye.

It is not easy to account for this difficulty as

*The sources of light in a colour-organ of 13,000 candle power*

to rapidity at the outset, as it is quite clear that our eyes are accustomed to rapid changes of colour under ordinary circumstances. The rapidity of change in a tumbling sea under a brilliant sky is extreme, and yet we enjoy it thoroughly. So also is the rapidity of alteration of colour in moving objects and yet we can appreciate it; and in an express train the eye finds little difficulty in watching the rapid changes of colour presented to us by the landscape as it flies past us.

My early experiments led me to think that the difficulty was really due to alteration of intensity or luminosity of colour, rather than to that of tint or character of the colour, and it occurred to me that the effect of this alteration of intensity upon the eye might be greatly lessened if the colour-field upon the screen were surrounded by a background of pure white light. This acted successfully to a great extent, and in the newer forms of instrument two vertical bars or stripes of strong and pure white light are placed upon each side of the colour-field and opposed by black.

Experience has shown that in a very short

time displays of mobile colour awaken a rapidly increased desire to see more of it. There is no colour either in nature or elsewhere of quite the same kind either as to its variety, strength, or delicacy, and to those who love colour—or perhaps even still more, to those who have a latent sensitiveness to colour of which they are almost unconscious—the new art opens up an entirely new field of pleasure and interest.

The first impressions received being, as already noted, those of the beauty of the colour and of its variety, there usually follows after this the demand, as in music, for a kind of rhythm in the colour composition. The player, for instance, gives us a passage of warm tints, of orange and rose colour, succeeded by cooler contrasts. The eye and mind then seem to demand a return to, or echo of, warmer colours. Or, if we translate this into time, if a composition opens with several long-drawn chords of colour succeeded by rapid phrases, there is a tendency in most people to desire to return to the balancing of effect of further slow and single chords.

*Part of the "action" of the inner diaphragms for giving intervals of relevant strength in the colour for each octave.*

The regular beat of a composition in well-marked time can easily be felt in colour, and time plays a far more important part than one would have supposed likely or possible in colour composition. To some extent it seems to take the place of form, that is, form in the sense in which the artist uses the word, though form as understood by the musician is certainly also felt in mobile colour.

The author has made many experiments with regard to the introduction of form, as the painter understands it, in the colour projected upon the screen, and has come to the conclusion that if used at all it should be indefinite or merely decorative and not in any sense realistic. The kind of form, for instance, which we see in cirrus clouds, while very beautiful in itself, has no definite meaning and is not calculated to distract the mind from the beauty of the cloud colour and yet is sufficiently interesting in itself. This kind of form introduced into the colour perhaps gives an added interest to it in slow compositions, but in rapid ones the eye and the mind have quite enough to do to appreciate and enjoy the colour itself without the addition of form, which would seem to be an unnecessary complication. The whole question of the introduction of decorative form is, however, a very interesting one and might well be explored farther. In music we are perfectly satisfied with compositions which do not express definite ideas, and in colour there seems to be no reason why this should not also be so if our colour sense is sufficiently developed. If stringed instruments had never been invented, could it have been for a moment supposed that a whole audience would sit spell-bound under the sounds produced by drawing a horse-hair bow over a tightened gut-string without definite words or ideas attached to such sounds? It is simply the insufficient training of the colour sense in many people that makes them demand form in addition to colour, or prevents them from enjoying colour for its own sake.

## CHAPTER VIII

### THE COLOUR SENSE AND ITS DECAY

THE decay of the colour sense has been referred to already, but it may be as well for us to consider the subject a little more fully, for if this decay is occurring it forms an important part of the plea for the further development of a pure colour art.

There is, I believe, some danger of the need for a better education of the colour sense being overlooked or under-rated, because many of us are unaware of the extent to which it has deteriorated and is deteriorating, and because we happen to be in contact with cultured or artistic people amongst whom there has been a slight revival of the feeling for colour.

It is perfectly true that a certain improvement in colour as used in house decoration and furniture has taken place, and that the scope of that improvement has somewhat widened.

But it still remains relatively small, and the great majority of the lower middle and working classes are not only absolutely inartistic in their tastes, but, as far as colour is concerned, incapable of appreciating good colour to an extent which it is difficult for some of us who have always lived in the art world to realize. Let us beware of concluding because we hear much talk in drawing-rooms or country houses about what is, or is not, artistic in colour, and much positive assertion upon the subject, that there is any widespread revival of the capacity for appreciating fine colour. Any such complaisant belief will be rudely shattered if almost any twenty people be taken at random and their feeling for colour be put to practical tests, or if we leave the average British workman to carry out the simplest piece of colour decoration upon his own initiative. This applies to most other European countries with nearly equal force, and we shall understand the position better, and see more clearly what we have lost and what are a few of the possibilities we are drifting away from, if we compare this state of feeling about colour, firstly, with what it was in the Middle Ages; and secondly, with what it still is in many Eastern countries.

If we go back to mediæval times we find good colour everywhere in pictures, mosaics, and illuminated manuscripts, in the costumes of the people, in stained glass and decorative frescoes, in pottery and textiles; and in these and other things there is evidence of its having been present amongst all classes. Do we not continually return to the art works of these great colour periods and study them with care and reverence, while our best artists are almost hopeless of excelling them in refinement and strength? Does not the glass of Chartres, Le Mans or Fairford, or that of so many of the great German and Spanish cathedrals, not only excite our highest admiration, but our envy; and is it not rare for our most skilled colourists to reach the colour harmonies of the craftsmen who produced the enamels of Limoges, the mosaics of St. Mark's, Ravenna, Monreale or Cefalu? Can we compare, with any satisfaction, the average decorative coloured fabrics produced in Manchester, or other of our manu-

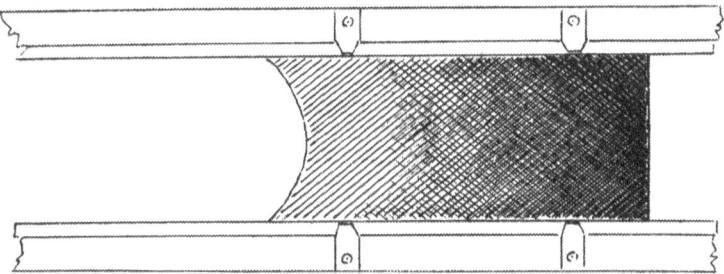

To show the construction of the diaphragms for giving *piano* and *forte* effects. The diaphragms consist of transparent mica crossed by innumerable lines which break up the light more at one end than the other.

firstly, with what it was in the Middle Ages ; and secondly, with what it still is in many Eastern countries.

If we go back to mediæval times we find good colour everywhere in pictures, mosaics, and illuminated manuscripts, in the costumes of the people, in stained glass and decorative frescoes, in pottery and textiles ; and in these and other things there is evidence of its having been present amongst all classes. Do we not continually return to the art works of these great colour periods and study them with care and reverence, while our best artists are almost hopeless of excelling them in refinement and strength ? Does not the glass of Chartres, Le Mans or Fairford, or that of so many of the great German and Spanish cathedrals, not only excite our highest admiration, but our envy ; and is it not rare for our most skilled colourists to reach the colour harmonies of the craftsmen who produced the enamels of Limoges, the mosaics of St. Mark's, Ravenna, Monreale or Cefalu ? Can we compare, with any satisfaction, the average decorative coloured fabrics produced in Manchester, or other of our manufacturing towns, with the exquisite woven materials which were once common throughout Europe, and which still linger in a few out-of-the-way districts?

If we turn from European mediæval art to that of the East, we find the contrast with the present appreciation of colour in Europe—at any rate in the decorative arts—still more marked. Persia, India, Japan, and China have all had their decorative colour arts for centuries past, and they retain them to a great extent to this day. Eastern colour is not only strong and splendid, but is also subtle and delicate to an extent which we can hardly appreciate; and though here and there there may be a tendency for it, at the present day, to run into the stereotyped forms which descend from generation to generation without much change, this cannot be said to be so everywhere. The craftsmen of China and Japan are still able to design in colour, to obtain ideas from nature and transmute them into exquisite decorative colour schemes. If it be argued that the colour sense in Eastern nations has from very early times been stronger and better than in Western ones, surely the reply is that we should profit by their example, and endeavour to render our eyes as sensitive to colour and our minds as open to its influence as theirs ; that we should, in fact, make special endeavours to bring our appreciation of colour up to their standards of the past as well as the present. The artistic colour sense must have been gradually developed in them as in us, and we should study the mode of its development even though our modern Western surroundings, apart from unspoilt nature, may be ugly and colourless as compared with those of the East, and our opportunities for seeing and enjoying colour fewer. This very ugliness and absence of colour is the outcome of our neglect, and due to the decay or non-development of the colour sense.

It can scarcely be disputed that at the present day large numbers of people are almost entirely insensible to colour, living in the world without being conscious that nature is full of beautiful colour harmonies, and never stopping to ask themselves how much of the beauty and interest of the surroundings of life are dependent on colour, or in the least realizing that there is urgent need for cultivation of the colour sense.

It is not, however, necessary to press the point. Even if the opinions expressed are considered pessimistic or over-stated, it is better to see clearly our weak points than to under-rate them, and we shall at least lose nothing by being on our guard against the decay of the colour sense, whether it is, or is not, as serious as some of us consider it to be.

Turning to another aspect of the question, I think it can be shown that the possession of a refined colour sense is of far more importance to a nation than its possession of a widespread musical one.

The defence of this bold assertion—which will, it may be feared, raise the ire of many musicians—may enable us better to see the position.

I have not the slightest wish to disparage music, which to me is one of the greatest of the arts, and one of the greatest pleasures in life, but it is at least conceivable that we might live (as man did once live in the early centuries) without other music than that of the birds or streams, and it is evident that there are at present thousands of people who hear hardly a note of music from one year's end to another, so that music is not essential to life.

But unless we are blind, or colour-blind, it is impossible for any of us to escape the influence of colour, be it good or bad. No object of any kind (unless it be black or white) is without colour. It is everywhere in nature, most of whose beauty is chiefly dependent upon it. In land and sea and sky it is omnipresent and in ever-changing variety—it is in every house and street, in every room and garden and field. We are constantly under its action—beautiful or ugly, healthful or morbid. We cannot escape from it if we would.

Is it not certain, then, that as it enters so much into our surroundings we cannot safely afford to know nothing about it, or to neglect to study it intelligently and cultivate our feeling for it?

Not only is it on all sides of us in nature pure and simple, but it is also practically everywhere in man's handiwork. All he produces (unless it be sooty black or absolutely white) has colour, and to a very large extent that colour is within his choice, and depends on his taste and the degree of the development of his colour sense. He selects the colours for most of the things he makes, modifies the natural colour of objects in a thousand ways, and has, in fact, the choice between good and bad colour constantly presented to him, and cannot escape from that choice. Moreover, upon his sensitiveness to colour depends to no small extent the effectiveness of his investigations in many sciences and his capacity for producing work of various kinds.

He stands, therefore, in a relation to colour very different from his relation to music, of which, if he is indifferent to it, he need have little or none; and colour must therefore be of more immediate importance to him in his daily life.

The doubt will, however, at once arise in some minds whether, after all, this question of colour and the colour sense is really of so much importance — whether it does matter

To illustrate inharmonious contrast of blue and rose-red, rendered less unpleasant by intermediate colour.

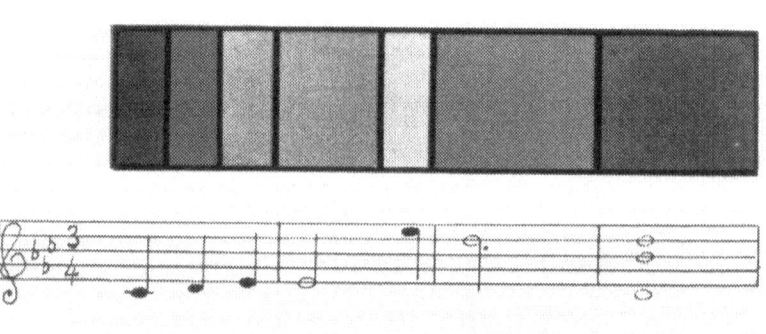

Example of a simple colour phrase in correspondence with musical notation.

NOTE. It must be understood that the colours are merely diagramatic, and give little idea of their purity as actually seen upon the screen.

much if we are surrounded by bad colour or not, or whether we do or do not neglect to train and develop our feeling for colour.

To these questions the following points may be submitted in proof of its importance :

Firstly : Neglect tends to degrade and destroy the great colour sense with which we have been endowed, just as disuse of any member of the body usually brings about its atrophy or disease.

Secondly : Because much in civilization besides art is dependent upon a widespread and refined colour sense, without which many channels of observation are closed. For example, delicate questions of colour enter into biological, chemical, and spectroscopic research.

Thirdly : Our intellectual and even our literary capacity is injured if we do not possess a keen sense of colour. Without it our great poets could never have written many of the best passages in some of their most imaginative poems, for to give only one instance—the delicate colour harmonies of sea or sky would never have suggested many a subtle metaphor or stimulated many a delightful phantasy.

Fourthly: The absence of a refined colour sense, as already pointed out, affects us very prejudicially in every kind of art, handicraft or manufacture into which colour enters ; and if, speaking from a national point of view, our capacity for colour falls below that of other nations, we shall not be able to compete with them in many of these.

Fifthly: It has been shown that colour has a direct influence upon health, mental and even physical, and this influence is probably greater than we have yet ascertained, and cannot be properly studied without the possession of the colour faculty.

Sixthly: Colour stands in a very similar relation to us to that which music occupies as a means of emotional expression, and the increase in the happiness and interest of life due to music will probably find a parallel in the pleasure and interest derivable from colour.

The importance of the retention and development of a refined colour sense being admitted, two further questions at once arise : firstly, whether it is possible to develop the colour faculty by education in the individual and in the race ; and, secondly, whether colour-music has any such educative influence.

As to the first of these questions. It is sometimes asserted that it is impossible to develop the musical faculty in those who do not possess it, that without a natural talent for music a musical education is of very little use. When we come to examine this assertion, however, we find that it is but a half-truth. There are doubtless persons who, having no musical ear whatever, can by no possibility be taught to appreciate music, much less become musicians. But for the majority of people, starting with some slight appreciation of music, it is quite certain that much can be done by education to develop their pleasure and interest in it. We know that this is so, and were it not most of our study of music in schools and colleges would be useless. The recent improvements in the musical education of children upon new aural methods have also proved it.

*Apparatus used for producing spectrum and obtaining position of colour intervals or "notes."
The box for enclosing the arc-lamp has been removed in order to show the latter.*

Turning from music to colour, there are of course those who are colour-blind, and there are many intermediate stages between total colour-blindness and a full sensitiveness to all the colours upon the spectrum-band. But the majority of people unquestionably have a certain appreciation of colour, even though it be slight or latent, and experience has shown that it can be increased and refined by education. Almost every artist realizes this. He knows from experience that the pictures he has seen and admired in which colour plays an important part have had an educative influence upon him. He knows that his study of nature has had a similar influence, and it cannot for a moment be denied that as a rule those persons who are brought up in artistic surroundings become more sensitive to colour and are less satisfied with the crude combinations which are sufficient to please the uneducated.

In America the education of the colour sense in children has been much more systematized than it has here. There are several excellent handbooks upon the subject, and the results obtained in elementary and other schools have, I believe, been very satisfactory. In Germany, and here and there in England also, systematic training in the matching of colours and distinguishing between tints varying very slightly has also shown a movement in the right direction.

Passing from the general question of the possibility of this education—as to which there can be little difference of opinion—we now have to consider whether colour-music has any such educative influence. This is, of course, purely a matter of experience, and it can only be stated in general terms that experiment has shown that it has such an influence. The more the eye is trained to notice very slight differences of tint in colour, the more sensitive does it become to these differences. In colour-music not only is an immense variety of tints presented to the eye, but the changes in these tints are often very rapid. At first they are not fully appreciated, but in course of time the eye gradually learns to follow and to enjoy the rapidity of change, and it also becomes more sensitive to very slight differences of combination. On general grounds also it may be reasonably argued that the use of any faculty tends to strengthen and develop it; and it is therefore probable, if not certain, that an art devoting itself entirely to colour would, and must, develop the special faculty to which it appeals. There can, in fact, be very little doubt that the art of mobile colour does stimulate and strengthen the colour sense even in a comparatively short time, and, were it in more general use, its effects and influence would of course be wider, and therefore the contentions as to its importance in this respect on general grounds would seem to be well founded.

## CHAPTER IX

### THE EMOTIONAL INFLUENCES OF COLOUR

THE reference in the last chapter to the emotional influences of colour brings us back to the original contention that not only is a pure colour art possible in theory, but that in practice it has wider capabilities and power of education than can easily be realized.

It is difficult for many people, however, to understand that colour can be enjoyed and appreciated apart from form in at all the same kind of way that musical sound can be enjoyed in music. How, they say, can you isolate colour and produce it apart from form and make it interesting or beautiful? In reply, let us go to Nature for examples of how she does something of the same kind.

There are few people who cannot admire a sunset. Yet in many sunsets there is little form, and in some there is none. The lower expanse of a cloudless sky may, for instance, be suffused with primrose, orange or crimson, slowly changing either as to depth and intensity, or in respect of its actual colour. The latter may perhaps darken through tints of amber into blue and violet, or fade into pale peacock-green and ashy grey through endless subtle gradations, and yet cloud-forms may be entirely absent. But who shall say that such a series of colour harmonies is without beauty or interest?

To take another instance from nature. In a wide expanse of sea there may be little form —if we exclude a certain amount of structure to be seen in the nearer waves or ripples—and the beauty of its effect often depends almost entirely upon its colour, fluctuating in intensity and full of texture, but appealing to us mainly as colour alone. Yet how exquisite may be the varieties of tint in almost any given space of it, with gradations and interweavings of green and turquoise, deep blue and violet, with sparkle of pearly grey and depths of dark indigo and purple.

Many other examples from nature might be

given, but these two will suffice to show that colour can be appreciated in nature for its own sake apart from form ; and, upon reflection, most people will admit that even under these conditions it acts upon us emotionally.

Even when a sunset has beautiful form as well as beautiful colour, it is usually the colour that strikes most people and remains in their memory, and produces the chief emotional impression.

The writer recalls a sunset at Ruta, near Genoa, to which this would probably apply, and it may also serve as a further example of nature's compositions in mobile colour.

As the sun sank across the Bay of Genoa the sloping mountains of the Riviera, clad with olives, accentuated by rocky peaks, and with the pale white towers of towns and villages scattered along the coast-line, were all bathed in a warm golden glow of sunlight. The sea was a liquid peacock-blue shot with green and violet, and the long line of the more distant Maritime Alps, stretching out across the horizon, told against the sky in a tender shade of greenish blue.

The effect thus began with a harmony in subdued gold and blue. As the sun neared the horizon, cloudlets formed above the distant peaks of the mountains and arranged themselves into those subtle fan-like groups which are often so exquisite in form and colour. At first these were of a pale dove colour, deepening from minute to minute and accentuating by contrast the light behind them. High above them appeared a few fleecy strands of vapour which soon drifted into delicate rose-coloured filaments continually changing their shape and gradually overhanging the lower fields of colour with a lace-like canopy across the whole width of the sky. Meanwhile the glowing light upon the nearer mountains and woods had been shut off and they had sunk into a tender green-grey, warmed in places by feeble tones of umber and madder. The distant mountains remained of the same deep peacock-blue, but the sea began to assume that strange rare colour of wine which is sometimes described by the Greek poets.

The first chord of this evening symphony of colour had given place to a series of others in which grey and rose were contrasted with grey-green, and in which the purple of the sea seemed as if it were a somewhat disturbing accidental note.

Further changes then took place, and the sky behind the mountains and the dove-coloured clouds became of a lemon tint streaked with topaz which gradually turned into a cool cinnamon, while glowing lakelets of aquamarine appeared in the lower sky. Meanwhile the topmost cloud filaments, far overhead, were deepening in colour, and from pale rose had become crimson, while the background of pure sky had changed almost to violet gradating downwards into paler tones.

Finally the splendour of the upper colouring faded away and the crimson filaments became a dusky grey touched here and there with a faint flush of pink. The sea darkened, and lines of current showed themselves upon its surface in cooler tones. The horizon on the other hand became suffused with ruby light, and the far-off mountains stood out sharply against it like the lead lines of a stained-glass window. Everything then deepened rapidly, and at last there was only one note of dull vermilion amongst the dying chords of grey and umber.

I think it may fairly be claimed that this, like many another sunset, was a piece of natural colour-music, and that it was well calculated to act on the emotions and to lead the mind from impressions of joyful beauty to the restful peace of night, though unlike the compositions of the colour musician it could never be seen again in all its fulness and variety. No doubt some of its impressiveness may have been due to the place and the poetic ideas associated with it, but how much less impressive would the whole scene have been under the glare of the midday sun or without the colour harmonies which have been described. It cannot, in fact, be denied that colour has an emotional influence in nature as it certainly has in pictorial art, and our own experiences, as well as the investigations of the psychologist, go to show that that influence is to a considerable extent independent of form.

If, then, colour in nature both with and

without form is interesting and beautiful, and if we are able by means of the colour-organ to obtain somewhat similar effects to those in nature, it may be argued as probable that we could arouse emotions of a similar kind. This is found from experiment to be the case ; and the next question is how far these emotional influences can be extended, and whether they can be made to assist in educating the colour sense.

It may be safely asserted that hardly any two persons are equally sensitive to the action of colour upon their eyes and minds ; and, in testing the effects of colour-music upon various people, this appears in a very marked way. We find, of course, exactly the same thing with regard to music. There are some to whom music is the keenest joy in life, others to whom it is a moderate pleasure, others who are indifferent to it, and, finally, those who will candidly tell you that it is a pain to them.

It might, therefore be expected that colour-music would be variously appreciated by different people, and this has proved to be the case. For some of those who see it for the first time there is a good deal about it which it is difficult for them to understand or appreciate, while there are others who find keen enjoyment and interest in it from the beginning. But it has been found that, within broad lines, the emotional effects produced by given passages upon different people are similar. That is to say, a colour-phrase of well-marked emotional tendencies will induce the same kind of mental attitude in various people. But, as in music, when we get away from these broad divisions of effect, the emotional results of less marked passages are much more uncertain.

There is one difficulty which has to be faced from the first, namely, that the full emotional effect of mobile colour upon the mind cannot be obtained without use of the contrast between slow and fast passages. But unfortunately, as has been said, in most cases, a spectator to whom mobile colour is a new, or nearly new, experience, cannot follow fast changes without considerable difficulty, and certainly cannot properly appreciate them. His eye is uneducated and puzzled. From this it will be easily understood that there are certain difficulties in showing effects of mobile colour except of an elementary description to untrained spectators. The appreciation of colour-music, however, rapidly develops after a few days' experience of it, but education and explanation are absolutely necessary at the outset.

Something has already been said about the expression of pathos and of joyfulness by means of colour, but it may be well here to give an example. Any sequence of colour which changes gradually from brightness and purity into depth of tone and greyness will, by general consent, be more or less pathetic. It is quite true that into this change enters the mere alteration of tone as distinct from tint, or, in other words, of light and darkness as opposed to colour. That is, however, also the case more or less in music, and it is difficult, if not impossible, to separate tone from tint in questions of emotional expression. But the very fact that the adjective "sad" is constantly applied to colour shows a general recognition of the fact of some colours being less suggestive of joy and brightness than others. Upon the instrument itself it is easy to show colour passages which have a pathetic tendency, and it is equally certain that phrases which are thoroughly suggestive of brightness and pleasure can be given, while between these two extremes lie rich fields of intermediate emotional possibilities.

To take an extreme example of emotional expression in colour, let us imagine a low-toned tint of dark purple which is slowly varied by successive chords of cooler and cooler colour until the purple has gradually changed into a deep blue with indefinite fluctuations towards absolute blackness. Now let us imagine a few short notes of half-developed red, then one blaze of deep crimson, and then a return to absolute darkness with faint suggestions of the previous purple and peacock-blue. I do not think that such a passage would have any other significance for the majority of people if its emotional effect were analysed than that of theatrical tragedy, though, as in music, this significance will always remain an indefinite and disputable one.

Speaking generally, the popular idea that low-toned colours are less exciting than bright ones, is borne out by mobile colour experiments.

As in nature, iridescence produces some of the most beautiful results in colour-music, and in rapid passages iridescent contrasts and harmonies affect the mind more than slow successions of plain colours or chords. These iridescent effects can be obtained in various ways—for example, by breaking up the component colours by diaphragms before they reach the screen, or by the surface of the screen itself, and very rapid successions of colour notes also produce the impression of iridescence.

If we examine a natural object which has iridescent colouring—for instance, the surface of some shells, or a piece of iridescent glass—we shall, I think, be led to the conclusion that great part of the beauty of the colour depends upon the minute contrasts contained within it. Red shades off into violet or green, in extremely small streaks and bars, and the violently contrasting colours are not large enough in quantity to be disagreeable—for quantity is an important element in questions of colour contrast—and yet they are sufficient to be exciting to the eye and the senses. Iridescence in nature always attracts us, and excites pleasurable emotions. We invariably admire it in the sunlit spray of the torrent, the plumage of the bird or the wing of the dragon-fly—and colour-music gives us the power of bringing it into being at our will and using it as an æsthetic influence.

## CHAPTER X

THE EDUCATIONAL INFLUENCES OF COLOUR-MUSIC

SIDE by side with the advantages of the new art as a wholesome emotional stimulus like music are its educational effects upon the colour sense. It is very remarkable to note how rapidly it produces increased sensitiveness to slight divergencies of colour, and how, after a short time, the eye can appreciate these differences much more quickly.

At first in any rapid passages of mobile colour most of the slight changes are scarcely felt at all, and it is only after a week or two that those compositions in which they most appear begin to give the greater satisfaction. Primarily it is the strong contrasts and the vivid colour combinations which most appeal to people, while later the delicate and subtle passages produce the greater impression and are more keenly enjoyed. In music, of course, we find the same thing, though perhaps not in so marked a degree.

There is also another side to the matter. Hitherto colours have chiefly been produced by mixing them on the palette or in the dye-vat, or in some other more or less laborious way ; their production has also been, to a considerable extent at any rate, dependent as to their range and variety upon the character and scope of the pigments used. With the colour-organ, however, an almost infinite variety of colour combinations can be obtained with no more trouble than in sitting down to the keyboard and running the fingers over the keys, and a vast variety of very exquisite tints are obtained with ease which it is extremely difficult and often impossible to produce by paints or dyes. Among these colours are thousands to which no name can be given, many of which one has never seen before, and the memory for colour is exercised in endeavouring to retain some recollection of them. Not only, therefore, is the colour sense rendered more sensitive, but the memory for colour is also trained, and in any art dealing with colour the memory plays a very important part. It is, in fact, to a large extent, due to the absence of a strong memory for colour that a great deal of modern decorative and imaginative art work leaves so much to be desired, as is now generally admitted amongst artists.

If the decorative painter has not got a well-developed colour memory, he will be unable to retain the impressions of beautiful colour harmonies which he sees in nature, and make use of them in his designs. Even in a direct transcript or study from nature the memory comes into play, for effects change from moment to moment, and the mere observation of a colour and the attempt to mix it on the palette is in itself an act of memory.

In watching the effects produced by the colour-organ upon the screen, slow and simple compositions should be studied at first; and as an exercise and training for the eye, it is a good plan for the observer to take the colours tint by tint and guess at the combinations which produce them, verifying them afterwards by reference to the keyboard.

The amount of pleasure and interest derived from colour compositions varies immensely with individuals. An interesting instance of this was the case of a well-known London doctor, who told the author, after first seeing a recital of colour-music, that he was absolutely unappreciative of any form of "sound-music," that it was, in fact, a pain to him, and that he had always detested it; "but," he said, "from the moment that I first saw a display of mobile colour, I realized what I had missed all my life through my inability to appreciate music. It opened up a new world of sensations to me and gave me the greatest mental pleasure I have ever experienced." This clearly shows that to some persons mobile colour would, or does, fill the place which music cannot occupy in their lives.

On the other hand, there can be little doubt that to some, though they would hardly own it, colour of any kind is more or less unpleasant, and they would prefer to live in a monotonic world. One must therefore be prepared for a great variety of opinions with regard to any such art as that of mobile colour.

The majority of people will probably derive a moderate but increasing pleasure from it. There are many to whom it at once provides a surpassingly interesting source of enjoyment and education, and some to whom, like my medical friend, it will open up an entirely new world of sensations; and there are others, again, to whom it will be supremely distasteful. It is well to recognize this to avoid disappointment, and be prepared for very divergent expressions of opinion about it.

Speaking broadly, it appeals most to those who have had an artistic training into which colour has entered, and it is less attractive to those whose interests centre in music. This is not what the author personally expected. He imagined that the connection with music being so close on some points, those who would take the greatest interest in mobile colour would be musicians; but, with some striking exceptions amongst distinguished musicians, the musical world, as far as it has yet come into contact with colour-music, has been at first inclined to see points of divergence rather than those of analogy and to look upon the art as a possible rival. A similar attitude is often adopted towards any new departure in science or art, and there is no reason for resenting it; it merely makes the co-operation of those amongst musicians who are able to take a sympathetic view and welcome the endeavour to open up new fields of investigation all the more valuable.

In some cases musicians, on the other hand, are very susceptible to the influences of colour. The German author Finck says, in reference to Wagner in the following curious passage, that "splendour, beauty, light, all the components of colour, were claimed by him as the rights of genius; from these in his life he gave in art the rich clangtones and tints which distinguish his music from all others. Wagner's love of colour in tones extended itself to his actual surroundings, and the influence of the glorious colouring with which he constantly surrounded himself is to be felt in every note of music he ever wrote. Catulle Mendes describes him as having been attired in coat and trousers of golden satin embroidered with pearls and flowers; for he had a passionate love for luminous stuffs that spread themselves like sheets of flame. Velvets and silks abounded in his drawing-room in broad masses and flowing pleats, anywhere, without pretext of furniture, without other reason than their beauty of colour, to give him the enchantment of their glorious brilliancy. Wagner fully realized the influence of these colour surroundings on his genius and his music, for he wrote, in a letter to Frau Wille, ' Is it really such an outrageous demand if I claim a right to the little bit of luxury I like; I who am preparing enjoyment for the world, for thousands? I am differently organized from other men. I must have beauty, colour, light.' "

With this testimony to the influence of colour upon the mind of a great musical composer, it is surely not too much to hope, or even to expect, that colour-music with its endless variety and magnificence of colour effects may well be of use in the future as a stimulating influence to musicians. Wagner's operas, as we all know, when they were first performed were attacked with insensate fury in France, and abused by the musical critics in England. If, therefore, colour-music should have aroused some slight opposition in the musical world, as well as have received some tributes of warm appreciation, there is no cause for surprise or discouragement. Wagner did not disdain to call in the assistance of colour both in his operas and in his surroundings, and were he alive now the writer believes that he would have found in him a warm supporter of some of the claims put forward on behalf of a mobile colour art. The educational effects of such an art are probably not confined to its action upon those into whose work or interests colour largely enters, but may well exercise an indirect psychological influence upon other arts of quite a different kind.

*Keyboard colour-organ as used in the author's studio.*

## CHAPTER XI

#### MOBILE COLOUR AND THE ARTIST

TURNING from musicians to painters, colour-music, of course, makes a much more direct appeal to the latter. To them the two specially new qualities in regard to this presentment of colour are, its separation from form and the introduction of time and rhythm. At first the absence of form makes the full appreciation of the colour somewhat difficult to them, every artist being trained to regard colour as occupying more or less definite spaces and shapes. But, on the other hand, the extremely subtle changes and interweavings of colour, the new methods of producing texture and quality, the rapid contrasts, the interesting changes of harmony, and the joy of being able to produce and study colour with the ease afforded by the colour-organ, makes them at once appreciative of the new art and more open to see its present and future possibilities than the musicians. Sir Hubert von Herkomer's remarks as to mobile colour will have been read with interest as bearing upon this point—all the more so, perhaps, from the fact that he is an able musical composer as well as a great painter.

An artist thinks little of undertaking a long and tedious journey in order to be able to watch and study the magnificent colour harmonies of southern seas ; the brilliant effects of sunlight upon the white buildings and costumes of Tunis or Tangier ; or to give himself the opportunity of making a few rapid transcriptions of sunsets only to be seen in the sierras of Spain or the deserts of Egypt. When, therefore, he is provided with an instrument by means of which he can study and analyse somewhat similar effects of colour at a moment's notice, he feels that a new power is placed within his grasp and appreciates its acquisition. It is first the technical qualities of colour that will most appeal to him. He is principally interested in the impressions produced by the interweaving of opposing colours and the resultant effects of luminosity and other beautiful qualities, and also by the æsthetic emotions produced by contrasts into which the element of time enters. Just as in a picture a contrast is largely influenced by the relative size of contrasting colour patches, or, in other words, by the relative masses of colour, so in mobile colour contrast is greatly modified in its effects on the eye and mind by the length of time during which the contrasting colours remain upon the screen. If, for instance, it is flooded with a deep red for a second or two, and a short sharp note of sapphire-blue is then struck, the contrast will be greater than that produced by two brief notes of scarlet and blue of equal duration. A whole series of rapid notes of colour of equal length which are more or less in contrast to each other affect the colour-senses less strongly than the same colours in contrast with others when of longer duration upon the screen.

Of special interest also to artists is the introduction of the element of time into gradated effects of colour by means of mobile colour instruments. In a picture or in a decorative design, gradation—that is to say, the gradual increase of the strength of colour over a given area—often occurs. In the works of the great landscape painters—such, for instance, as Turner, where the problems of atmosphere and space have interested him so greatly—gradation of colour is present almost everywhere. But it is, as it were, fixed gradation; it may begin slowly and may rapidly increase in depth and intensity over a given space until it culminates in a strong point or focus. Its rate of change may also be quite equal and steady with no rapid increase and no rapid decrease, but in both cases, once stated, it is fixed and definite, whereas when colour is produced by the colour-organ under conditions of gradation, whether it be towards intensification or of weakening of the colour, it grows, or wanes, under the eye of the spectator and can be quickened, or retarded, at the will of the executant. Gradation of colour under such conditions becomes much more interesting.

Mobile colour is also of practical aid to the

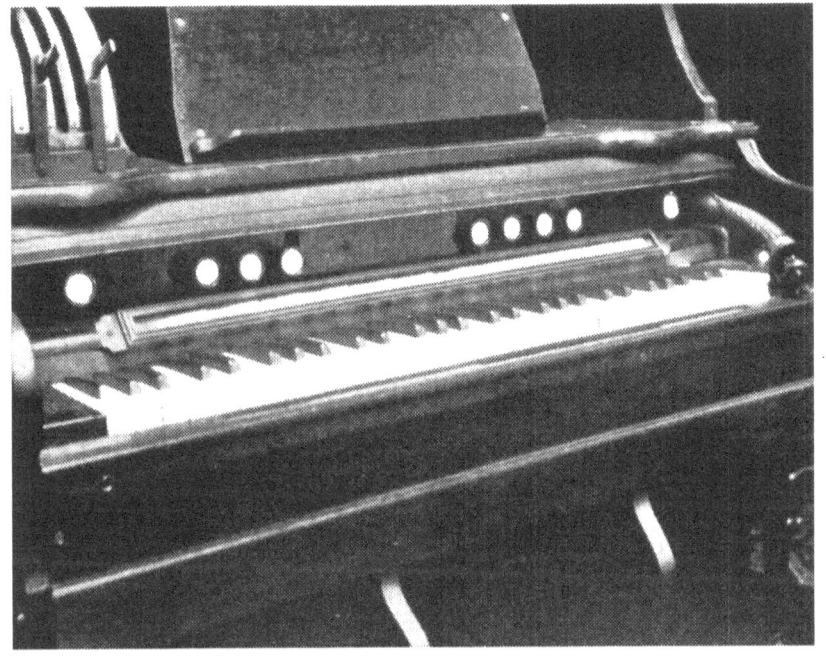

*Keyboard of a colour-organ.*

artist, because it enables him to try almost any scheme of colour he may have in his mind without the laborious process of transferring it to canvas or paper. He can sit down at the keyboard of the colour instrument, and starting from some chord of colour which pleases him can try various sequences of other colours and other combinations without the least difficulty. He can come back to his original chord and try fresh ones without having to clean his palette or provide a new canvas, and he can, at any moment, if he wishes to make a study of the effects he has decided upon, reproduce these colour schemes upon the screen and make notes of them before he begins his picture.

Many artists wisely keep objects of beautiful colour in their studios in order to be able to bring their minds into tune with the beauty of colour in nature or art. Some choose Oriental china, others Limoges enamel, others the plumage of birds or collections of gems and minerals, others, again, mediæval and oriental draperies or stained glass. But the artist who has access to a mobile colour pain produced by colour are much more pronounced, in most cases, with the artist than with the ordinary spectator, and it is therefore to the artist that the new art must look in the future, as it has up to the present time, for the greatest assistance in its development. Experience has shown that once having overcome the disconcerting realization of the fact that colour does not require form to make it beautiful or interesting, the eye of the artist becomes rapidly educated to appreciate the subtleties of colour-music.

A point that strikes most artists is that already alluded to, that however many colours are mixed upon the screen, there is no tendency towards deadness or impurity of colour as in the case of pigments. The greater the number of colours projected upon the screen, the greater the tendency towards white light; whereas in pigments, the greater the number of colours mixed upon the canvas, the greater the tendency towards blackness.

Vast numbers of combinations appear in colour-music which are seldom or never seen in art and very rarely in nature, and these are specially worthy of the painter's attention. One practical difficulty is that the colour appears in a darkened room, and can therefore only be compared with other tints produced in a similar way, and not with local colour of objects placed near the screen. But a special arrangement for comparison of the local colour of particular objects can be made by throwing detached beams of white light from an arc-lamp upon them. The two narrow bands or strips of pure white light usually projected upon the screen at each side of the colour-field also give a standard of comparison between the colours upon it and absolute white, and enable the depth and intensity of low tones to be better appreciated. If no such bands of light are used, low-toned colours, by reason of their being surrounded by darkness, are apt to appear too luminous, and their full strength cannot be realized. Somewhat the same conditions exist in stained glass windows in a dark church, and it was probably in order to enable the beauty of the sombre colours which the great stained glass designers of the Middle Ages often used that they frequently surrounded their pictorial designs by fields of white or grey glass. This is very marked in the windows at Fairford, and in much German glass, and the principle has been adopted by a whole school of modern English glass painters in imitation of them.

Another very important effect of the white bands is to prevent, as has already been said, the colour changes from becoming too dazzling to the eye and too violent in their effect. Their width is an important point and has to be found experimentally. If they are too wide, the brilliancy of the paler tints is injured; if, on the other hand, they are too narrow, the depth of the darker ones is not fully appreciated.

The use of the colour-organ in training the memory for colours may become important to young artists, many of whom neglect this training and regret it later in their careers. There are many people who have a keen musical faculty in other respects, but have no musical memory, and so there are many excellent artists who have a very feeble memory for colour, largely, perhaps, because they have not cultivated it systematically. Endless exercises in memory training for colour are possible with the colour-organ, and many interesting experiments in this direction have been made.

## CHAPTER XII

SOME SCIENTIFIC OPINIONS

CONSIDERING the question of the analogy between colour and musical sounds purely from the scientific standpoint, there is, broadly speaking, a general agreement amongst scientific men that there are some remarkable points of resemblance between the respective modes of being of the spectrum-band and the musical octave. In both, the sensations produced upon the eye and the ear are due to variations of frequency of pulsation in the air and the luminiferous ether respectively. But, starting from this broad general statement of fact, there are divergencies of opinion as to how far further resemblances extend, and the question has perhaps been additionally complicated lately by the wide acceptance of the electron theory. As long as we confine it to physical science the path for the investigator to follow is, as far as it will take him, a fairly clear one. Physical facts as to the production of colour and of sound can, within certain limits, be definitely stated and compared. But when we come to the consideration of the effects of colour and of sound upon our eyes and ears, and through them upon our minds and emotions, upon memory and association, and upon those springs of suggestion and mental impulse which are so closely connected with art, we are in an altogether different domain and one within which there must necessarily be almost endlessly varied opinions.

Amongst scientific men we shall therefore not be surprised to find that some attach considerable weight to the analogy between the spectrum-band and the octave, and the action of colour and sound upon us mentally and emotionally; and that others attach very little and endeavour to confine themselves solely to the physical outlook. We may, perhaps, go as far as to say that valuable and helpful as is the opinion of men of science with regard to the latter, it is to those who have been trained to observe and study the emotional effects of colour and sound upon us, and whose lives have been spent in experimenting upon these influences through the medium of their work—namely, to the artist, to the musician, and also to the psychologist—that we should turn for further assistance in investigating the difficult and interesting questions connected with our subject, many of which press for solution.

But, at the same time, it is of great interest to compare the opinions of various scientific men of eminence, and in this chapter it is therefore proposed to give a brief summary of some of these opinions.

The general points of resemblance between colour and sound struck the earlier men of science very forcibly, and there are numerous references to them in their publications. There is not, however, much profit in going back to these opinions, as the scientific outlook, even with regard to physical science, changes so rapidly; but the following extracts from the works of the earlier authorities of our own time may be of interest:

Prof. Tyndall wrote:

"The pitch of sound is wholly determined by the rapidity of the vibration. *What pitch is to the ear in acoustics, colour is to the eye in the undulatory theory of light.* . . . Nevertheless, this great theory of undulation, like many another truth, had to establish by hot conflict its rights and existence. Illustrious names were arrayed against it."[1]

In Ganot's *Handbook of Physics* occurs the following:

"The analogy between the phenomena of light and sound is very close. . . . A red light is due to a comparatively long undulation and corresponds to a deep sound; while a violet light is due to a short undulation and corresponds to an acuter sound."[2]

Prof. H. Schellen, in his well-known work upon *Spectrum Analysis*, states:

"Different colours are only produced by the different degrees of rapidity with which the ether vibrations recur, just as the various notes in music depend upon the rapidity of the suc-

---
[1] Prof. Tyndall, *On Light*.
[2] Ganot's *Physics*. Edited by E. Atkinson, PH.D., F.C.S.

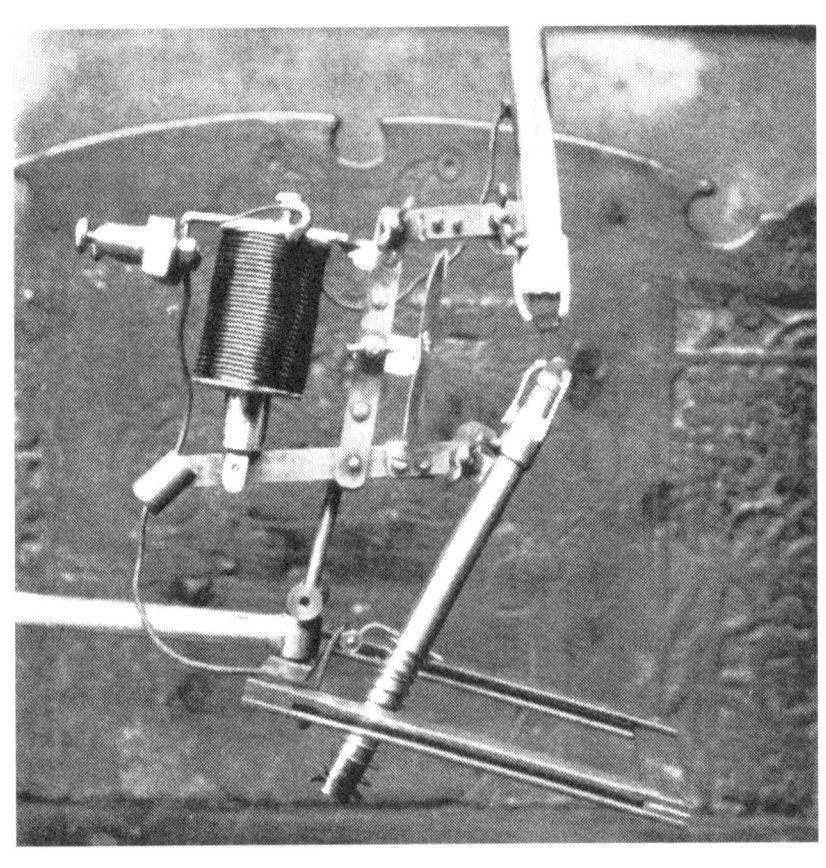

*One of the patterns of arc-lamp, specifically designed for mobile colour instruments.*

cession of the vibrations of air. Colours are to the eye what musical tones are to the ear."[1]

Or again, in Preston's *Theory of Light* the author writes:

"As the pitch (or musical colour) of a note is determined by the frequency of its vibrations, so it is the frequency of the vibrations in the luminiferous ether that determines the colour."

In the last edition of the *Textbook of Physics* by A. W. Duff (1910) the matter is still referred to thus:

"It is a matter of common experience that the colour of a beam of light does not change when it enters water, hence frequency rather than wave-length determines colour. Colour is therefore analogous to pitch in sound."

Professor Heinrich Rubens, the great investigator of the infra-red rays, would also appear to group them in octaves as a con-

[1] Prof. H. Schellen, *Spectrum Analysis*. Edited by Sir W. de W. Abney, F.R.S.

venient method of nomenclature; but I am not aware how far he considers the musical analogy to extend.

Professor R. A. Gregory, who tells me that he considers that the analogies between musical sounds and colour are remarkably close, makes the following statement with regard to the musical octave, which is exceptionally clearly put and may be of interest in any comparison between the two scales of colour and sound.

"The major diatonic scale, such as is represented by the sequence of the white notes of a piano, commencing with the middle C, is built up in the following manner: a second major chord is obtained by starting from $C^1$, the octave of C, and descending in the ratio 6 : 5 : 4. This gives frequencies of 48, 40, and 32; and these correspond to the notes $C^1$, A, and F. This set of three notes is known as the 'sub-dominant chord.' Finally, a third major chord is obtained by starting from G, and ascending in the ratio 4 : 5 : 6. This gives frequencies of 36, 45, and 54; and these correspond to the notes G, B, and $D^1$. This is known as the 'dominant chord.' The note $D^1$ is above the octave of C, and its lower octave D, having a frequency 27, falls between C and E. Thus we obtain the following sequence of notes into which the octave may be divided :

| Notes | C | D | E | F | G | A | B | C |
|---|---|---|---|---|---|---|---|---|
| Vibrations per second | 256 | 288 | 320 | 341·3 | 384 | 426·6 | 480 | 512 |
| Frequency | 24 | 27 | 30 | 32 | 36 | 40 | 45 | 48 |
| Interval (compared with C) | 1 | $\frac{9}{8}$ | $\frac{5}{4}$ | $\frac{4}{3}$ | $\frac{3}{2}$ | $\frac{5}{3}$ | $\frac{15}{8}$ | 2 |

"[1]

Leaving the strictly physical side of the matter for a moment, the following observations by Helmholtz are interesting as showing that he felt the limitations of the older arts into which colour enters, and that they therefore occupied a totally different position from music and had less to do with what he calls "pure sensation." They almost suggest regret at the absence of any art using colour for the purpose of influencing the emotions in a similar way to that in which music uses harmonic sounds:

"Music stands in a much closer connection with pure sensation than any other of the arts. The latter rather deal with what the senses apprehend, that is, with the images of outward

[1] *A Classbook of Physics*, by Prof. R. A. Gregory, p. 345.

objects, collected by physical processes from immediate sensation. Poetry aims most distinctly of all at merely exciting the formation of images, by addressing itself especially to imagination and memory, and it is only by subordinate auxiliaries of a more musical kind, such as rhythm and imitations of sounds, that it appeals to the immediate sensation of hearing. Hence its effects depend mainly on psychical action. The plastic arts, although they make use of the sensation of sight, address the eye almost in the same way as poetry addresses the ear. Their main purpose is to excite in us the image of an external object of determinate form and colour. The spectator is essentially intended to interest himself in this image and enjoy its beauty; not to dwell upon the means by which it was created." [1]

Many modern painters would not entirely agree with this limitation of the scope of painting, and it has become the fashion to refer much to the means by which a pictorial effect is produced in present-day art criticism, but, nevertheless, Helmholtz' contention is in the main a true one, that music has hitherto stood

[1] Helmholtz, *Sensations of Tone*, p. 2.

alone as an art in its close connection with pure sensation, and that the other arts being more or less tied to the expression of form and definite ideas cannot use colour in the same kind of way as music uses sound.

Dr. G. D. Macdonald published an interesting book some years since upon " The agreement of the musical and colorific scales," and stated, *inter alia*, that " the inference is therefore legitimate that if the analogy of the musical scale were taken as a guide, the special points of the spectrum whose respective vibrations would compose a well-tempered diatonic scale of colour may readily be chosen."[1] This, of course, is matter of opinion, and I give the statement with all reservation.

Professor Grove was also struck by the closeness of the apparent relation between sound and colour, and, though the artistic possibilities of the use of colour in similar ways to sound did not strike him in reference to the subject, he said in his *Correlation of Physical Forces* that " the analogies in the

---

[1] *Sound and Colour*, by Dr. G. D. Macdonald, F.R.S.

progression of sound and light are very numerous."

To summarize briefly. The physicist rightly confines his attention to the physical facts to be observed with regard to the production of colour in the spectrum and in other ways, to theories concerning the nature of light and colour, and to deductions which may be drawn from their physical phenomena, and to what they can tell us with regard to the sources from which they emanate and their chemical, electrical, and other material effects. He experiments upon sound in a similar way and considers it from a like standpoint, and he notes points of physical analogy between the two sets of phenomena, but he leaves the intricate question of the effects of colour and sound upon our senses and our minds to the biologist and the psychologist, as also the deductions which they may draw from their observations. Harmony and discord, contrasts and blending in sound and in colour are, for instance, questions directly concerned with the impressions produced upon us, are complicated by various psychical considerations, and are therefore more or less outside the domain of physical science. The latter with its clear and unbiased vision gives us its invaluable assistance up to a certain point, but there it leaves us, as to this question of colour sensations and their mental influences, to pursue our own experiments and make our own deductions.

## CHAPTER XIII

### REMARKS UPON CRITICISMS AND APPRECIATIONS OF COLOUR-MUSIC

IN this chapter it is proposed to consider some of the points which have arisen during the long series of experiments made in mobile colour, and also to give a brief summary of some of the critical and other opinions from outside sources.

These two classes of opinions and criticisms are, of course, very diverse both in character and value. The small group of musicians, artists, and others who have followed or taken part in the experiments carried out personally by the author, and have watched the construction and reconstruction of the colour-organ and similar instruments, have been in a very much better position to discover weak points and appreciate strong ones than those who have merely been present at one or two public lectures where it has not been possible to enter into long explanations or discussion of the objects aimed at, the questions at issue, and the difficulties which have had to be overcome. With the former these could be talked over as they arose, and from time to time alterations could be made in the mechanical construction of the instruments, and the principles on which they have been designed could be revised, so as to take advantage of fresh experiences and criticisms.

With regard to articles upon the subject there has been much intelligent appreciation of the views put forward, and but little of the hostility which usually greets a new departure. It was quite inevitable that there should be some misconceptions, both as to the theories advanced and the results to be achieved; but by reprinting portions of some of the articles that have appeared the opportunity is afforded of clearing away some of these misunderstandings, and I therefore propose to adopt this course.

Before doing so, however, it may be as well once more to state the position claimed for colour-music.

The first and most important contention I have put forward has been, and still is, that there is a broad general resemblance between the effect produced upon the mind and the emotions by colour and by musical sounds. Going further, I, with many others, consider that with both colour and sound this general resemblance in emotional effect is largely dependent upon proportion and contrast coupled with harmony and dissonance, that this makes the general analogy still closer, and that there are other important points of resemblance. Whether, or how far, the physical analogy between the spectrum-band and the octave holds good or has its counterpart in sensation, is, it may once again be said, a secondary matter and one open to question, but on broad lines I submit that the deeper points of resemblance between the effects of colour and musical sounds upon us are so strong that they cannot be disputed by any unprejudiced person, though the support of this contention must depend to a great extent upon actual experiment and demonstration, and it is unavoidable that the question should be complicated by variations in individual capabilities of receiving emotional impressions, either from music or from colour.

Quite apart from any resemblance to or dependence upon music, a mobile colour art has a *raison d'être* and firm and solid foundations upon which it can be built up, as already contended elsewhere.

Returning now to the main subject of this chapter, the first impressions received from colour-music are as a rule those of the varying beauty of the colour itself, with which for the time being the eye is satisfied, without the mind attempting to analyse the sequences of colour or to inquire whether any method is behind the effects produced.

This would seem to correspond to the stage in the appreciation of music in which all that is demanded is something pleasant to the ear, and in which an untrained auditor is unable to take in the details or the deeper musical significance of a serious work.

The next step is usually that of the recognition of colour phrases, of the repetition of these in varied form, and of there being a general intention or structure in a colour-music composition.

Curiously enough, experiment has shown beyond possibility of doubt that for most people a colour composition which has been based or modelled upon an already existing musical one is more interesting and produces finer effects than most original compositions. I do not wish to attach any undue weight to this, as it is probably owing to the fact that mobile colour has yet to find its great composers, and that the experience required to write original colour compositions has yet to a large extent to be acquired, but it is a strong argument for using musical precedents as a temporary assistance.

When the colour phrase as shown upon the screen becomes easily grasped and recognized, the next demand made by the eye and the mind appears to be for some sort of predominant tendency in the colour—for something which, figuratively speaking, might correspond to "key" in music, but which would also partially include other general characteristics of a musical work. As in painting, a colour composition may be either warm or cool in tendency, or with strong or merely delicate transitions and variations. It may also, for instance, be written in a general key of some one particular colour which is predominant throughout, and in which contrast is very sparingly used, or it may be greatly broken up and with rapid alternations of contrast.

Contrast is more demanded at first and less later on, and there are many other points of this kind which are of interest, but into which it would be tedious to enter at any length in the absence of actual demonstration.

One of the difficulties with which mobile colour has had to deal is that of wide fluctuations of luminosity in the compound tints, and various mechanical devices have been designed and experimented with in the construction of the instrument in order to overcome this. To a large extent it has been now avoided, and it has been found that extreme and disagreeable alternations in luminosity are chiefly due to ineptitude in composition or extemporization.

Turning for the moment from the results of actual experiment to outside criticisms, it has been asserted that one difficulty with which colour-music has to deal is, that the eye is incapable of appreciating changes of colour as rapid as the changes of tone which occur in music. If this were so, it would merely be an argument against the direct translation of rapid sound-music compositions into colour-music. The art of mobile colour does not, however, make such translations or adaptations one of its chief objects, and it might, in fact, abandon them altogether and yet leave its main purposes untouched.

It is, moreover, demonstrable that, so far from the eye being unable to appreciate changes as rapid as those which the ear can follow, its capacity is much greater in this respect. In photography it is found impossible to design a shutter so rapid in its action as to enable the most sensitive photographic plate to seize the image of some very rapidly moving bodies. These are therefore sometimes exposed in the dark, and illuminated for an infinitesimal portion of a second by an electric spark of a duration far shorter than that of any musical note. If we take two such electric sparks of different colours and allow them to appear in a darkened space, the eye will, notwithstanding, be perfectly capable of distinguishing between their respective colours. No musical note at all approaches an electric spark as to its shortness of duration, and therefore the whole contention as to the inferiority of the eye in this respect falls to the ground. This, however, should be frankly admitted, namely, that rapid colour changes are at first fatiguing, and that to appreciate them in colour-music requires some training and experience. At first there is a sensation of dazzle, but, as previously stated, this gradually disappears, and is after a time, with most people, entirely lost. So much so is this the case that, as pointed out, the preference for slow compositions soon gives place to the desire for more and more rapid ones.

A difficulty that occurred to the mind of a musical critic was that in music the high notes, namely those of rapid vibrations, are cheerful and light; while to him the more pleasing and exhilarating colours, such as red, have the lowest vibrations. In reply it may be said that this is a purely personal impression and cannot be taken as a normal one. In the construction of the forms of colour-organ provided with a keyboard, the upper octaves are paler and lighter than the lower ones. If, therefore, there is anything in the contention that cheerfulness and light are intimately associated, that association is taken account of in the arrangement of the colour scale in these instruments. But, as a matter of fact, few people would agree with this critic in thinking that low-toned reds such as are found at the red end of the spectrum-band are the most cheerful colours. Nothing is much more cheerful and exhilarating than the strong or opalescent blue of the sky or of many flowers.

With regard to this point, in the careful researches which have been carried out in Germany as to the relatively pleasant effect of different colours upon the eye, satisfactory results could of course only be obtained by taking averages from a large number of people, and in the present stage of education, or rather of ignorance, with regard to colour it is quite impossible to found any arguments upon isolated instances of preference for individual colours, or, even taking a wider view, upon those attaching to one end of the colour scale or the other.

Another critic who evidently felt the initial difficulty of appreciating rapid colour changes wrote in an excellent article upon the subject: " For those—and they are many—who love colour for its own sake, the new art seems to offer endless possibilities of pleasure, and their only grief will be that each beautiful colour is only seen for a short moment before it is succeeded by another." He went on to say that, " though the training of the last few thousand years or so has enabled us to detect tune in sound, we are as yet unable to detect it in colour." We have already discussed rapidity of change and its advantages, and with regard to "tune" it may be said that a melody is nothing more than a pleasing succession of notes arranged in some rhythmical order, some shorter, some longer, some pleasant in sequence, some less so. In colour it is quite possible to have the same kind of arrangement, and many persons can, even at first sight, receive pleasure from such a colour phrase or melody, and can remember it perfectly. Both the power of recalling it and the pleasure of seeing it are, of course, rapidly increased by education of the eye, and it is quite true that it may need a long period of time for average audiences to gain an appreciation of colour-music at all equal to that they now have of sound. This is, however, not an argument against the art, but rather one in favour of giving increased opportunities for studying it. The writer went on to say that he fails to see how emotion can be awakened " unless a distinct faculty for appreciating tune is developed"; but in colour, just as in music, experiment shows that an emotional impression can be produced even by a sequence of two or three notes, and it is probable that colour is much more independent of definite melody or tune than is music.

Turning from tune to form, some of those whose impressions of mobile colour effects I have tested experimentally feel in the first instance a certain uneasiness when form—that is to say, a space of colour of a definite and distinctive shape—is entirely absent. Seeing colour they seem instinctively to demand form also, though in a short time the desire for it lessens and finally disappears. This is but what might be expected. We are accustomed to associate colour with the shapes of objects, and at first it surprises and somewhat puzzles us to see it separated from them and presented to us for its own sake. Then after a time, having our attention confined to colour alone, we begin to appreciate it more and more, and to realize how beautiful and impressive it may be apart from any form whatever.

But this initial difficulty has to be faced and will always recur at first, and we must not only be prepared for it with those who are new spectators, but also with the larger number of persons who only hear or read descriptions of colour-music. How, they ask, can colour be interesting without form? And all that can be said is that actual experience of it is the only satisfactory reply to the question.

It would seem that what really take the place of the additional interest which form gives to fixed or stationary colour are the elements of change and of rhythm which a mobile colour system introduces.

The increase in the desire for rapid changes contrasting with slower ones, already several times referred to, seems to point to this conclusion, and form, in the sense in which the musician uses the word in speaking of a musical composition, gradually enters into or attaches itself to the colour in the mind of the spectator.

There will always be a certain number of people who perhaps having little natural liking either for music or for colour—or who, caring much for music, have little feeling for other forms of art—will ask whether mobile colour has any "practical objects," or whether it can be turned to any "practical use." They ask this in all sincerity and with no desire to be hypercritical. The question has, to a certain extent, already been dealt with, but may be answered rather more fully here. The art of mobile colour stands in the same kind of relation to the practical side of life as music or painting occupy. It cannot actually produce a pattern for a fabric or a subject for a picture, but it can stimulate and develop the senses and faculties upon which the ability to design in colour depends; and better than this, it can bring a new source of interest and refreshment as well as a refining influence into life, just as music has done.

Any art that develops the faculties which enable mankind better to enjoy and appreciate the infinite beauty of nature is worth cultivating, and it is impossible to say to what its study may lead, or for what useful purposes it may not ultimately be turned to account.

One or two writers, in referring to my early lectures on the subject, whilst admiring the beauty of the colour effects produced, and admitting the plea for the development of a mobile colour art, were nevertheless of opinion that it should not be associated with music. Their grounds appeared to be, firstly, that they did not admit closeness of the musical analogy in some respects—a point I have fully dealt with elsewhere—and that they considered it unnecessary to associate colour with music in order to enhance and increase the emotional influence of the latter upon the hearers or spectators.

This view is based upon a misapprehension. I have never asserted or thought that all, or even most, forms of music would gain by being associated with or accompanied by mobile colour. My contention has been, and still is, that mobile colour, if not always used as a separate art, may with advantage be associated with music in compositions in which each gives and sacrifices something in order to produce a combined art, and occasionally also may be used as an addition to already existing musical works, which seem to allow of this. There is a very obvious precedent for this in opera, in which the musical score sacrifices something to the words and action, and, on the other hand, the latter concede a good deal to the music, so that a co-partnership is established of mutual benefit. I think upon reflection it will be admitted that there is a good deal to be said for a similar co-partnership between colour and musical sound.

Another of the writers referred to made a curious criticism. He said : " Music is absolutely an art of proportion, the charm of a chord consisting of the proportions to one another of vibration of its component notes. A quick ear always feels a note as a vibrating tone and can soon be trained to detect the different components of simple chords. Does any painter, even the most competent, recognize vibration as part of colour ? Could he resolve a compound colour with certainty into its components, saying at once which of these components was quickest in vibration ? Can our enjoyment of colour be shown in any way to be due to a sense of vibration ?" To this it may be replied that in every picture, in every decorative design, in every colour pattern, the question of proportion of the colour tints and the colour masses enters, and also that any artist can determine almost at a glance what are the tints and what are the pigments, and the degrees of strength which build up any given space of colour in a picture.

As to vibration in colour, a whole school of painters endeavour to express their sense of the vibratory origin of colour by technical processes which emphasize it, so much so that some few have even called themselves Vibrationists.

A certain number of criticisms resolve themselves into various forms of expressed doubt as to whether the asserted analogy between colour and music holds good at all points. In the previous chapters of this book I have entered somewhat fully into this question; but it may be here restated once more that I do not consider the analogy to be a close one in every respect, however certain and important it may be in others. If it were precisely similar at all points, there would, in fact, be less to be said for the development of this new form of art. If colour were completely analogous or identical in its effects upon our minds to those produced by music, there would be little advantage in using it for such an art. But it appeals to another sense capable of stimulating similar emotions upon which an art somewhat resembling music can be built up—but arousing other interests, developing other faculties, and opening up other possibilities.

The disinclination of some to allow that colour should be put into partnership with music has already been referred to; but there are others, again, who seem to feel that the chief emotional use for mobile colour will be in illustration and emphasis of musical compositions. It has nevertheless been asserted by one writer that, though this association of the two arts seems desirable, "the eye can grasp but an octave of colour, while the more delicate and complex ear possesses some ten thousand fibres, each vibrating in sympathy with the musical note. The pitch and intensity of a sound may be arbitrarily represented in colour, but what about the qualities of tone? This third attribute of a note or chord finds something wanting in the sister science."

In reply to this, it may be said again that, as a matter of fact, the number of tints appreciable by the eye exceeds by hundreds of thousands, perhaps millions, the number of tones appreciable by the ear. It is quite true that there is only one octave of colour, but the intercombination between the component colours of that octave in the vast ranges of tones they possess, gives us the almost endless variety of colours which we see in nature and in art, whereas it is scientifically demonstrated that the tones appreciable by the ear are not at all comparable in their number to these.[1]

The second objection as to quality of tone in music not being represented in colour opens up an interesting point. *Timbre* in music is produced by the admixture, greater or less, of harmonics with the ground-note which is being sounded; or with each of the notes composing a chord. If the vibrations of air producing a given note are recorded by an optical curve by means of a suitable instrument, with a needle attached to a sensitive diaphragm which traces it upon a smoked glass, these harmonics clearly show themselves as small notches or wave crests upon the main line of the pulsations of the diaphragm, being

[1] See reference to this in the chapter upon the psychology of the subject.

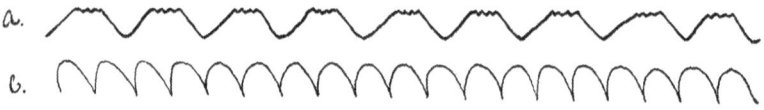

TO ILLUSTRATE "TIMBRE."

The upper line (*a*) shows curves produced by a musical note with *timbre* harmonics, the lower line (*b*) those given by a tuning-fork nearly free from harmonics.

as it were the ripples upon the surface of a wave.

In colour we have, as a matter of fact, somewhat similar harmonic interruptions. If a particular colour is taken, say a general tone of rose colour, and its texture is broken up by slight tendencies to violet, to warmer red or to orange, an effect is produced upon the eye which may be said to be analogous to that of *timbre* in music. An absolutely pure colour thrown upon the screen, or made visible in some other way, may be taken from one point upon the spectrum-band, and will then correspond to an absolutely pure musical note without harmonics. But nearly the same colour sensation, though an enhanced one as to beauty and interest, may be produced by slightly altering the original ground tint and breaking into it with almost imperceptible streaks, dots, mottlings, or texture-producing marks of other divergent colours, in such a way as to give the same general impression as did the original colour yet with a different texture. This in pigments is a process well known to the artist, and he relies upon it for some of his most beautiful colour effects. *Timbre* in music corresponds, in fact, somewhat nearly to " quality " or texture produced by harmonious or divergent tints in the case of colour.

## CHAPTER XIV

### SOME FURTHER REMARKS AND SOME PAST PROPOSALS

IN various articles which have appeared upon colour-music reference has been made to cases of what are commonly called "colour-hearing"; that is to say, to instances of persons who, on hearing a given note or a particular phrase in music, always have a strong mental impression of a particular colour or set of colours. Cases of this kind are established facts, and have been referred to again and again by various well-known philosophic writers and psychologists, amongst others by Locke and Nussbaum. Little attempt has, however, been made to tabulate or systematize them, and no writer upon the subject, so far as I am aware, has yet shown that for the same notes similar colour-imaginings or sensations are aroused in various people. It would seem rather that the colours suggested are more or less arbitrary, or perhaps derived from some obscure associations, and therefore the subject has not much interest for the student of colour-music except in one important respect, namely, as a further piece of circumstantial evidence of there being some closeness of origin or common foundations in the senses and in the brain upon which, as it were, the emotional or psychological influences of colour and sound are based.

These associations of certain colours with certain sounds may perhaps have given the first impulse to some of the ideas as to a possible relationship between colour and music to which occasional reference may be found in early literature. Probably the earliest suggestion of an analogy (as distinguished from the possibility of a separate art) was made by Aristotle in the following passage :

"Colours may mutually relate like musical concords for their pleasantest arrangement; like those concords mutually proportionate."

The idea of an independent colour art somewhat analogous to that of music has also crossed a few minds at intervals during the past centuries. Since some of my earlier experiments I have made diligent search in the British Museum and elsewhere for any records of these ideas, but literary evidence of them is very sparse, and it is only within comparatively recent times that there have been more than very fragmentary or obscure allusions to the subject.

The first account I can discover of an attempt to give practical form to the conception of a colour art occurs in the following disjointed description, written from the somewhat amusingly hostile musical standpoint of the time :

"Lewis Bertrand Castel, a Jesuit of Montpellier, whose 'Physical System' ranks amongst the best philosophical works of the early part of the eighteenth century, studied vision and the nature of colours, as blended or contrasted with each other, till his imagination getting the better of his understanding he confounded the eye with the ear and associated the harmony of tints with that of sounds.

Infatuated with this idea, he invented what he called an Ocular Harpsichord, which was strung with coloured tapes instead of wires, and being placed in a dark room, when the keys were touched the transparent tapes, which respectively corresponded with them, became visible ; and the various successions and combinations of colours, consequent to this operation, produced effects on the sight, which his fancy assimilated to the impressions made on the ear by melody and harmony."[1]

After this curious attempt to show a correlation the subject seems to have again dropped into obscurity.

Coming to more recent speculations, an interesting book upon *Sound and Colour* was published by Dr. G. D. Macdonald, F.R.S., and there exists a pamphlet by the late Lady Archibald Campbell entitled *Rainbow Music, or the Philosophy of Harmony in Colour Grouping*. She employed what she considered to be the analogy between the octave and the rainbow for suggestions for the decoration of a room

---

[1] *Assimilation of Colours to Musical Sounds*, by Dr. Bushby. Published 1825.

for which, amongst other materials, to obtain her colour combinations, she used coloured shells.

Professor J. Perry's experiments in Japan have also already been referred to. He and Prof. Ayrton designed an apparatus for determining the effects produced by a spot or spots of coloured light made to move in lines or curves upon a screen.[1]

The following remarkable forecast in reference to a possible mobile colour art, which appeared in the Rev. H. R. Haweis's *Music and Morals*, was brought to my attention when completing my first experiments:

"Colour now stands in the same kind of relation to the painter's art as sound amongst the Greeks did to the art of the gymnast. But just as we speak of the classic age as a time long before the era of real music, so by and by posterity may allude to the present age as an age before the colour-art was known —an age in which colour had not yet developed into a language of pure emotion, but was

---

[1] If any further experiments by others should have taken place, particulars of these would be welcomed by me.

simply used as an accessory to drawing, as music was once to bodily exercise and rhythmic recitation. And here I will express my conviction that a colour-art exactly analogous to the sound-art of music is possible, and is amongst the arts which have to be traversed in the future, as sculpture, architecture, painting, and music have been in the past. Nor do I see why it should not equal any of these in the splendour of its results and variety of its applications. Had we but a system of colour-notation which would as intensely and instantaneously connect itself with every possible tint, and possess the power of combining colours before the mind's eye, as a page of its music combines sounds through the eye to the mind's ear—had we but instruments, or some appropriate art mechanism, for rendering such colour-notation into real waves of colour before the bodily eye, we should then have actually realized a new art, the extent and grandeur of whose developments it is simply impossible to estimate. . . . But what a majestic symphony might not be played with such orchestral blazes of incomparable hues ! What delicate melodies composed of single floating lights, changing and melting from one slow intensity to another through the dark, until some tender dawn of opal from below might perchance receive the last fluttering pulse of ruby flame, and prepare the eye for some new passage of exquisite colour! Why should we not go down to the palace of the people and assist at a real colour prelude or symphony, as we now go down to hear a work by Mozart or Mendelssohn?"[1]

The colour organ and allied mobile colour instruments have, to some extent at least, realized the hopes expressed. It should be added that Mr. Haweis afterwards took a keen interest in the results obtained, and his death deprived the new art of a strong supporter and eloquent champion of its claims.

Shortly after one of my first demonstrations of colour-music, an article of considerable interest, by Mr. William Schooling, appeared in *The Nineteenth Century*, to which the editor added a footnote stating that it had been in his hands for a year or two. Mr. Schooling's views, therefore, were formed quite independently of my own, and are consequently

[1] *Music and Morals*, p. 32.

the more valuable in support of the general theory of a mobile colour art, though, as I had been carrying out experimental work for some years previously, and had discussed various points involved with many friends, it is not impossible that some of these may have reached the writer through indirect channels. Mr. Schooling asked the following questions:

[1] "Is it possible to create an art that shall appeal to us in a kindred way to music, and to educate our perceptions so that we may appreciate the melody and harmony of sound? The analogy of colour to sound is one consideration that may lead us to think that we can perhaps answer 'Yes.' Objectively, and as a matter of physical science, the two are so far alike that both are wave-motions, though of different kinds; the pitch of a sound and the colour of a light are both dependent on the number of vibrations; violet light and high notes result from frequent vibrations; red light and low notes from comparatively few vibrations, and probably, though not of necessity, they would arouse similar sensations.

[1] Reprinted by kind permission of the proprietor of the *Nineteenth Century and After*.

The thunder of a storm might conceivably be represented by low notes and red colour, the lightning by high notes and violet light.

"The range of audible sound comprises about eleven octaves, the range of musical sound about seven; the range of visible light is less than one octave; the range of artistic colour may perhaps be less, as in the case of sound; but the seemingly narrow limits of colour to less than one octave is more verbal than real, for if we consider that the limits of musical sound lie between 40 and 4000 vibrations in a second, while the limits of visible light lie between 460 millions of millions and 680 millions of millions in the same time, it would seem probable that a larger number of colours and tints could be appreciated by the eye than notes by the ear, and that, therefore, the variation producible by combination of colours is greater than the variations possible by musical combination into chords, while the change from tint to tint could be incomparably more gradual and delicate than the change from note to note. But how far it would be possible or desirable to have scales of colour starting from different points and with intervals between the tints or colours, dependent on certain proportions between their respective vibrations, I am not prepared to guess."

Mr. Schooling went on to describe a possible colour-music instrument in the following terms :

" The first to suggest itself is naturally a series of vacuum tubes or vacuous chambers that could be had in any desired variety, that could be illuminated in succession or combination by the use of a keyboard, on playing the notes on which the electric current would pass through different tubes. Contacts would be made so easily that the most elaborate chords or combinations of colours could be played with the utmost simplicity, and the intensity of the light, corresponding to the loudness of sound, could be varied, as in a piano, by using a pedal to alter the intensity of the current, so causing the tubes to shine with a brilliant light or to glow in the softest of hues."

I think some interesting results might be obtained with an instrument of the kind suggested, though so far as I know none has been constructed; but by its means separate colours only, or at most groups of separate colours, could be produced and not compound tints, which would greatly limit its range. Any fresh proposals, however, as to new principles for the construction of colour-music instruments are to be welcomed. The points raised by Mr. Schooling as to the wider scope of a mobile colour art as compared with music are of special interest, and the notes (see p. 173) as to the immensely greater sensitiveness of the visual nerves as compared with the aural give much support to these contentions.

## CHAPTER XV

### COLOUR-MUSIC AND PSYCHOLOGY

SO far as men of science are concerned it is quite clear that it is to the psychologist that colour-music, or any form of mobile colour art, will be especially interesting ; and it is chiefly to the psychologist that we must look for assistance in analysing the impressions which are produced by colour-music. To Dr. William Brown, of King's College, London, I am much indebted for assistance in exploring the psychological outlook, up to the present time, upon colour and its sensory and emotional influences ; and in view of his valuable contributions to psychological science the note in this book to which his name is attached will, I am sure, be read with interest.

The physicist can tell us much that is valuable as to the constitution of light, the production of colour, the rate of vibration in the luminiferous ether which corresponds to a given colour, the points of resemblance and dissimilitude between colour and sound, and various other matters of the highest importance.

The biologist can take us a step further and help us to understand the action of light upon the nerve terminations of the retina behind the lenses of the eye, and he can follow the tremulous air waves of music for us up to the point of their impingement upon the basilar membrane of the ear, and perhaps even a little further. But the object of colour-music is to make an appeal to the mind and the emotions, to the mental sense of colour, and to its intellectual or emotional effects upon us; and when we come to these questions we have to part company with the physicist and the biologist and enter the domain of psychology.

As a matter of fact, up to within the last few years psychology has unfortunately investigated the subject but little. One may almost say that the emotional effects of colour are only just beginning to be studied, and it is one of my hopes that colour-music will give a new impulse to further investigations, and to obtaining additional records of experimental facts upon which we may be able to build in the future.

There are many questions which careful psychological experiment might be able to answer for us, such, for instance, as—

(1) How far similar colours affect the majority of people in a similar way? This investigation has been commenced in Germany by Professor Exner, but only with regard to single colours. As I have already mentioned, he experimented upon a large number of people, chiefly as to their choice of what they considered the most beautiful colours, and upon some points he obtained great unanimity of opinion. But he discovered, and quite frankly admits, that contrasts of adjacent colour at once upset most of his conclusions.

This brings us to another important question for psychologists, and one which I would venture to suggest for their further consideration, namely—

(2) What are the influences of contrast in

colour, what are the normal or average limits of agreeableness in contrasts, what are those of discordancy, and what, on the other hand, are those of harmony?

On these points individual opinions are of little value. Experiments must be spread over a large number of persons of varying education, and perhaps also of race, and the hasty conclusions which have been arrived at by many writers upon colour theories should from the outset be re-examined and the whole question considered anew.

Some past theories with regard to colour, such, for instance, as Goethe's, and even those of great experimentalists like Young and Helmholtz, have had a cramping influence upon psychological investigation, valuable as have been many of their contentions or suggestions in other respects.

An entirely new set of questions for the psychologist are, in addition, opened up by the introduction of the elements of time and rhythm into colour, which it is now possible to study by means of colour-music instruments. Such questions, for instance, as—

(3) What counterpart does rhythm in music find in colour?

(4) Does education of the colour sense by means of the rhythm introduced by colour-music tend to evolve an increased demand for colour rhythm in the majority of persons?

(5) Can rhythm in colour be with advantage more complex than in music?

Other interesting points for consideration are:

(6) Upon what conditions do tragic, pathetic, and joyful emotions evoked by colour depend, and do they upon broad lines coincide in different people with similar colour effects?

Dr. W. Brown is of opinion that music creates a set of emotions different from and apart from our ordinary emotional experiences, and evolved, as it were, in a higher plane of our consciousness. He agrees with me in thinking that these, though different in character from what may be called normal emotions, nevertheless assist in stimulating the latter, and it seems probable to me that the same view holds good with regard to colour-music effects, and that indefinable emotions are produced as well as those to which we can put some sort of name. It is probable that if this is true, part of the stimulating, helpful, or restful effect of music is dependent upon these super-emotions as we might call them, and this opens up a most interesting field of inquiry.

There are many other points which might be suggested as suitable for psychological study and investigation, with the help of a mobile colour art. Meanwhile, it may be interesting to give a few short extracts from psychological writers who have dealt with colour.

In *Music—its Laws and Evolution*, by the eminent French scientific author, Monsieur Combarieu, the following passage occurs: " We will point this out by taking for a brief comparison two given realms—music and light. The two senses to which they correspond, the eye and the ear, alone receive impressions which systematize themselves into a work of art. Smell, taste, and feeling, though susceptible to the highest education, and in no way limited to a utilitarian part, have not given rise to creations of a truly æsthetic character. To show the analogy between sound and light, music and colours, will be to realize, on an essential point, the problem of harmony we have traced out."

This is a portion of an argument in favour of the unity or similarity of action of colour and sound upon us, and the writer goes on to say: "Are the two senses of hearing and of sight formed by the same evolution and by a similar process? This is what the facts of history would seem to affirm."

So far as physiological investigations have been made upon points of analogy between the action of colour and sound upon us, they would seem to support very strongly the general contention of the analogy being a close one.

With regard to the question of the effect of rhythm in colour, some very valuable experiments have been made by Dr. B. Berliner, which he records in his work *Der Ansteig der reinen Farbenerregung in Sehorgan*. He there states that "a rhythmic movement or repetition of colours in varying intensities produces the maximum effect of sensation upon the optic nerve, and hence upon the mind." This I have found to be corroborated by experiments in colour-music.

The same writer considers that he has proved that various colours have similar degrees of power in exciting particular sensations even under varying conditions of lightness or darkness of the colours.

Other experiments upon this question have also been carried out by the psychologist Arthur Mitzscherling.[1]

Before accepting these conclusions as to the effect of degrees of lightness or darkness, we should have to understand exactly what the experimenter means by sensations. Results obtained from colour-music would seem to show that lightness or darkness has a great deal to do with the impressions obtained from given colours.

Elsewhere reference has been made to one great difficulty which at once presents itself in

[1] *Die Farben-Kurven bei Reduktion auf gleichen Helligkeit.*

comparing a musical note with its corresponding colour upon the spectrum-band when similarly divided, in that the whole construction of the diatonic scale is very arbitrary, and that it is inevitable that any colour scale must also be so to some extent.

In reference to the diatonic scale and the use of musical precedents for mobile colour purposes, the following remarks by Dr. Max Meyer in a paper on *Elements of a Psychological Theory of Melody* are of interest as showing the dissatisfaction which many feel as to the non-scientific and unrepresentative character of the diatonic scale in music. After remarking that there are plenty of books on musical theories written by professional musicians, physicists, physiologists, and others—but that in his opinion the psychological laws upon which music is founded have not yet been determined—he goes on to say : " The wrong path, much frequented, which inevitably leads back to the starting-point, is the adoption of the theory that the basis of all music is the so-called diatonic scale, represented by the numbers 24, 27, 30, 32, 36, 40, 45, 48. . . . This so-called diatonic scale which is the basis of all discussions in Helmholtz's *Tonempfindungen* was introduced into the modern theory of music by Zarlino in 1558. It was accepted by Rameau in his *Traité de l'Harmonie*, 1721. According to Rameau (and Helmholtz) no numbers play any part in music except 1, 2, 3, 4, 5, and 6. This is certainly not a law derived inductively from observed facts, but a dogma, because one may, as Poole rightly states, very easily observe that the 7 acts psychologically in a way corresponding to the action of 2, 3, and 5; whereas, indeed, with other prime numbers, as 11, 13, etc., this is not the case. . . . There can be no doubt that the tempered scale cannot be made the basis of a theory of music, that theoretic conclusions drawn from considerations regarding the interval of the tempered scale have no scientific foundation. A scientific theory of music can only be a theory describing the laws of music performed in just intonation, but in just intonation that *really* is to be called 'just,' not in that *seemingly* just intonation of Helmholtz, which—as can be proved by experiment—does not deserve this name." This dissatisfaction with the diatonic scale and its inconclusive construction, as already said, complicates the whole question of similarity between the two scales.

Schopenhauer in *Die Welt als Wille und Vorstellung* fully recognizes the immensely important position which colour occupies, or ought to occupy, in relation to human life and civilization, and develops his views in many eloquent passages ; but he naturally regards the whole question from the philosophic and not from the practical point of view.

Some interesting observations have been made by E. Bullough in *The Perception Problem in the Æsthetic Appreciation of Single Colours*, but they are mostly too abstruse to be of much assistance in attacking the questions to which a mobile colour art gives rise. As a matter of fact, many of these break entirely new ground, and special investigations are required to explore them.

To sum up. Psychology has only just begun to explore the emotional effects of colour, but in the main its conclusions, so far as they go, are highly favourable to the general theory of colour-music and tend to support the contentions that a mobile colour art has serious and important claims upon our attention.

# APPENDIX

THE following comparative table of visual and auditory sensations will be of interest as showing some of the points of resemblance and difference between these. It also opens up further questions for future investigation.

## COMPARATIVE TABLE OF VISUAL AND AUDITORY SENSATIONS

### Some Points of Resemblance and Difference

| Visual Sensations | Auditory Sensations |
|---|---|
| 1. *Physical stimulus*, produced by transverse waves in the ether between the limits of 440 billion vibrations per second and 770, approximately.<br><br>Change set up in the sense-organs a chemical one.<br><br>The vibration-frequency of extreme violet approaches twice that of extreme red at the opposite end of the spectrum. | 1. *Physical stimulus*, produced by longitudinal waves in the air between limits of 20 and 22,000 per second (varies in individuals).<br><br>Change set up in the sense-organ—the basilar membrane—is probably physical.<br><br>Any audible wave-frequency being doubled comprises between these extremes the musical sensations contained within the octave. |

| Visual Sensations | Auditory Sensations |
|---|---|
| 2. Hue, saturation, and intensity are dependent in the main upon wave-length, wave-complexity, and wave-amplitude respectively. | 2. Pitch, timbre, and loudness are dependent in the main upon wave-length, wave-complexity, and wave-amplitude respectively. |
| 3. A series of greys extending from white to black are due to a mixture of rays of all wave-lengths. <br><br> Non-neutral greys are due to predominance of some rays of particular wave-lengths. | 3. Noise, as distinguished from musical tones, probably due to a mixture of all tones. <br><br> Noises may differ in pitch. This is due to predominance of certain tones. |
| 4. From a physiological point of view well-marked turning-points in the spectrum are at yellow, green, blue, and red. | 4. Salient points in the musical scale—in order of closeness of physiological relation to the fundamental tone—are octave, fifth, fourth, major third, minor third and sixth. |
| 5. Colour mixtures or fusion of colours. | 5. Combination tones, interruption tones, beats, etc. |
| 6. Simultaneous colour contrast. <br><br> This occurs usually when two or more colours occupy visibly separate spaces in proximity to each other. | 6. Tonal fusion, or the sensation produced by a number of notes in a united chord or noise. <br><br> Ebbingham follows Stumpf in considering that it is a characteristic |

| Visual Sensations | Auditory Sensations |
|---|---|
| But it may also occur when these spaces are so small as to be separately indistinguishable, as in the case of many colours in flowers or insects, or in three-colour photographic processes, and this would seem to correspond to some extent to tonal fusion, i.e. a number of notes combined in a chord. | peculiarity of hearing that it is possible to distinguish individual tones in a combination—"die allgemeine Fähigkeit eine objectiv zugleich vorhandene Mehrzahl von Tönen auch subjecktiv als eine solche zŭ erkennen." But this distinction seems somewhat artificial, the real difference being that whereas the constituent tones do not occupy separate spaces, in the case of contrasting colours they must do so. |
| 7. Successive colour contrast—including "after images." (Successive contrast is an important feature of colour-music). | 7. Less marked than in colour, but as to "after-images" a similar effect probably occurs in the realm of sound, but of very short duration. The question has yet to be explored. |

If the spectrum and the octave be divided into similar intervals in accordance with the diatonic scale, the following table shows the approximate frequencies of relative vibration and the relative colours corresponding to each note or interval. The verbal description of these colours is, however, of course an inadequate and inaccurate one. Colours, like musical tones, cannot be properly described in words. Greenish blue, for instance, may mean any one of many thousand shades of the colour with varying tendencies towards green and blue.

It is also nearly, if not quite, impossible to represent pure spectrum colours by means of pigments. Any diagrams in this book into which colour enters must therefore, like the following table, be taken merely as approximate statements.

TO SHOW DIVISION OF COLOUR SCALE UPON KEYBOARD COLOUR-ORGAN WITH MIDDLE C CORRESPONDING TO LOWEST RED OF SPECTRUM

| Approximate ether vibrations Mil. mil. per sec. | 395·0 | 433·0 | 466·0 | 500·0 | 533·0 | 566·0 | 600·0 | 633·0 | 666·0 | 700·0 | 733·0 | 757·0 | Invisible |
|---|---|---|---|---|---|---|---|---|---|---|---|---|---|
| Approximate colour | Deep red | Crimson | Orange-crimson | Orange | Yellow | Yellow-green | Green | Bluish green | Blue-green | Indigo | Deep blue | Violet | |
| Musical note | (Middle) C | C♯ | D | D♯ | E | F | F♯ | G | G♯ | A | A♯ | B | $C_1$ |
| Vibrations per sec. | 256·0 | 277·0 | 298·0 | 319·0 | 341·0 | 362·0 | 383·0 | 405·0 | 426·0 | 447·0 | 469·0 | 490·0 | 512·0 |

The subjoined quotations from articles upon colour-music are inserted here for the following reasons:

1. Because in the absence of ocular demonstration for the majority of readers of this book, it seems well to include some few descriptions of the effects produced upon entirely unprejudiced eyes and minds.

2. Because it affords an opportunity of making one or two further replies to criticisms which it seems fairer to quote verbatim.

In an article upon the subject, its author stated that "the keynote of the new art" was "mobility introduced into colour, enabling time, tone, and rhythm to be expressed in modulations." The keyboard of the colour-organ was described as being "like a palette on which all the subtle gradations of hue and tone are evolved but not fixed. Fleeting and momentary as sounds, the whole gamut of colour was thrown on to the screen in slow or rapid successions in infinite combinations . . . and in waves of intense and most lovely colour, the tints blending and neutralizing each other, and presenting subtle tones, taxing the eye to seize and follow them; now deepening into sombre hues, now passing into infinitely delicate gradations, and now bursting into full pure hues of surpassing beauty, the magic evanescent colour flitting across the vision in indefinable harmonies."

This is interesting as a description of the impressions made upon an unprejudiced person unknown to the author, who evidently belonged to those who, witnessing a demonstration of colour-music for the first time without any special training for it or experience of its possibilities, are yet able at once to appreciate and enjoy it.

In an article in *The Times* written after a demonstration of colour-music, after describing the effects produced and remarking that the tints with which the screen was filled were often very beautiful, the writer went on to say that "there is perhaps force in the suggestion that our eyes are not yet sufficiently practised to make us competent judges of colour as expressive of emotion; but it may be remarked that even were the physical analogy between sound and colour complete—which it is far from being—it does not follow that the emotional effects are analogous."

This is, of course, perfectly true, and the analogy has to be demonstrated. But to return to a question already somewhat fully discussed, the physical analogy in view of very similar physiological action through the nerves makes it probable that there would be similar emotional effects, and following upon this probability experiment shows this to a considerable extent, at any rate, to be so.

The following are extracts from another article:

"As concords and discords in proper relation and succession build up a musical structure to the ear, so they do to the eye. The trained ear anticipates certain successions of harmonies, and is held in suspense until the succession is completed. Likewise does the eye, artistically vexed for the moment by certain discordant combinations of colour, await in suspense the concord which must artistically follow."

The writer concludes with the following remarks: "Wherein the art differs from painting is, firstly, that the colours in their concord or discord are not necessarily associated with definite form. And, secondly, that whilst any picture, once painted, remains fixed in its single harmony of combination, the notes or colours of the colour-music flow successively one into the other, as if we could conceive a picture or a colour design in which the group or multitude of hues were constantly being replaced by others, under government of the same intellectual laws which regulate the musical successions."[1]

Many interesting articles have appeared on the Continent showing an intelligent appreciation of the subject, and the following curious extract from *Le Temps*, written in a vivacious and somewhat figurative style, may perhaps be read with interest:

"Dans l'exécution d'un morceau de musique, la succession des couleurs répond à l'agilité du doigté et au mouvement de la page écrite ; l'instrument donnant en tons la mesure, le rythme et l'harmonie du son.

"A la première rencontre c'est la surprise, un peu l'éblouissement qui dominent ; mais on s'habitue bientôt à discerner le coloris des maîtres, à reconnaître la pourpre de Richard Wagner, le bleu céleste de Mozart, les ors profonds et les rubis étincelants que charrie l'œuvre de Saint-Saëns ; et l'on conçoit

[1] *Yorkshire Post.*

peut-être de la page entendue une impression plus vive, plus facile et plus sincère.

"Il en resulte que, grâce au 'colour-music,' on ne doit pas désespérer d'arriver à donner une sensation musicale à un sourd de naissance. L'inventeur ne pense nullement que cette sensation soit jamais parfaite et complète, mais il n'est pas douteux que la vue de ces lumières rythmées, furtives, vivantes, fasse naître dans les esprits mûres aux sons des idées de cadence, de mesure et un sentiment d'harmonie générale dont il est facile de pénétrer le sujet.

"Le prélude de *Lohengrin* n'a point la même 'couleur' qu'un refrain populaire. Longtemps avant l'instrument dont nous nous occupons, la critique musicale se servait volontiers de ce mot 'couleur' pour rendre des effets que sa technique ne lui permettait pas d'exprimer avec une netteté satisfaisante ; mais Herold—qui usait volontiers de cette formule—ne soupçonnait pas sans doute que quelque jour un instrument mathématique traduirait cette couleur des maîtres pour nous montrer tous les soleils de la Crau dans 'l'Arlésienne' de Bizet, les horizons du Sahara dans le 'Désert' de Félicien David, des blancheurs de lis dans Gounod, des pâleurs d'aurore dans Léo Delibes, et des tempêtes, des gloires, des pourpres allumées, des embrasements de batailles dans une phrase de la Marseillaise qui passe.

"Quel peut devenir l'utilité du 'colour-music'? . . . C'est aux savants d'examiner, de mediter et de conclure. Un premier pas a été franchi dans une voie inexplorée, vers un but mystérieux."

This article, written some time since, of course lays far too much stress upon some of the experimental " direct translations " of musical writers which were then given, but as I have frequently explained, such translations, founded as they must be upon musical and colour scales, both of which are arbitrary although they show strong points of resemblance and produce very beautiful colour effects, are not the objective of colour-music.

## MUSIC AND COLOUR
*Recent Works on the Psychology of Music*

The following conclusions, quoted from a summary, by W. B. Pillsbury, of papers read at the Fourth Congress of Experimental Psychology at Innsbruck, in April, 1910,[1] are of interest in regard to some of the points already discussed in the body of this book :

" W. Kohler presents a suggestive note on the possibly discontinuous character of the tone qualities. His experiments grew out of the tendency to refer a vowel quality to certain pitches. In two subjects he found that a note of about 265 v.d. was similar to *u*, 528 to *o*, 1054 to *a*. The suggestion is that these sounds have the same relation to the musical scale that the primary colours have to the spectrum. In answer to questions he asserted that there was a quality lower than *u* that corresponds to the *m* sound, and probably others still lower that give critical points for sensational qualities as the vowel sounds do for the upper notes."

[1] From the *Physiological Bulletin*, Vol. VIII, pp. 210-11.

*Primitive Musical Scales*

"Messrs. Stumpf and Hornbostle reported on the results obtained from a study of the phonographic records of primitive music that the psychological institute at Berlin has been collecting. Prof. Stumpf discusses two conclusions that have already been reached. First the tendency to equal-interval scales of five and seven tones, second the widespread use of fifth and fourth relations in part songs. In the Javanese five-tone scale the notes are related $\frac{5}{2}$, the tones of the seven-note Siamese scale as $\frac{7}{2}$. These prove that the occidental scale is not the only relation that may be used in music. Stumpf rejects Wundt's suggestion that the scale has arisen from making the differences in the blocks of the zylophone or metallophone (the musical instruments used in Java) proportionately equal, for observation of the blocks show that they have been hollowed out in the course of tuning. It is evident that the tuning is by the ear rather than by the eye, and that the scales represent a maximum of beauty to the natives. On the problem of the harmonious relations of simultaneous tones, the author reaches the result, that the intervals of the octave, fourth, and fifth at first appeared by chance among a large number of other relations, and were selected and retained because they were the more pleasant on account of the close approach to the unison effect that makes the words more easily appreciated. These are only preliminary to the many results that may be expected from a careful study of phonographic records of primitive and other music."

The origin of and differences between musical scales are of importance in any consideration of the analogies between colour and music.

### Origins of Polyphonic Music

V. Hornbostle suggests other ways in which polyphonic music might originate. The antiphonic parts might easily overlap, first by chance, then be repeated intentionally when the effect was found to be pleasant; or the use of falsetto that is found in primitive music might, in singing with others, give a consonant effect with the voices of others and be repeated through its agreeableness. Possibly the interval of the major second that is found among the Admiralty Islanders might have been developed through the failure of some voices to sing in unison. He also remarks on the complexity of the rhythm and of the melodic structure of primitive music.

### The bearing of this upon Colour-Music

The history of the development of opinion amongst certain races as to what colours can be harmoniously combined would be of equal interest in connection with colour-music problems.

If this variety of scale, founded upon varieties of feeling, exists in music there is no cause for surprise at some divergency of feeling with regard to harmonious and discordant combinations in colour. A mobile colour art may well assist in bringing about more unanimity of opinion as to fundamental principles of harmony, and by its means experimental tests can be applied with great ease to large numbers of persons and the results tabulated and analysed. Such results may, and probably will, lead in the end to the construction of new colour scales to which the present forms of instrument could easily be adapted. They would also serve as the basis for new forms of mobile colour composition, and I have this object in view in present experimental work.

Musical scales and compositions must be founded more or less upon some general unanimity of opinion and feeling, amongst those to whom music appeals, as to what is beautiful in tone combinations and sequences and what is unpleasant, and the knowledge of that unanimity—which lies at the root of the art of the musician—has only been gradually acquired. Thus it must also be with colour. But it is only now—for the first time in the history of the uses of colour—that mobile colour instruments give a ready means of obtaining similar points of unanimity.

## A. Wallace Rimington
(1854-1918)

Alexander Wallace Rimington was a well known landscape painter, having studied in London and Paris, and was a Professor of Art at *Queen's College* in London where he taught painting and developed his *Colour-Organ* which he patented in 1894.

He wrote two books, *Colour-Music: The Art of Mobile Colour* and *Architecture Seen Through the Painters' Glasses*. His ideas on the relationship between color and music were adapted by Alexander Nikolayevich Scriabin, the Russian avant-garde composer, and used in *Prometheus: The Poem of Fire,* (1911). Rimington's *Colour-Organ* was used for its 1915 New York premiere.

www.ingramcontent.com/pod-product-compliance
Lightning Source LLC
Chambersburg PA
CBHW030136170426
43199CB00008B/93